Sporades Islands Greece.

Travel Guide

Author
Michael Lopez

INFORMATION-SOURCE. This book is strictly prohibited from any illegal or unauthorized digital or physical reproduction including photocopying, illegal distribution, Electronic/digital manipulation, without the prior written permission of the publisher. Information-Source publishing holds anyone failing to comply with the above mentioned responsible, and will be pursued under Copyright law.

Copyright © 2021 Information-Source Publishing
All Rights Reserved.

First Printed: 2021.

Publisher:
INFORMATION-SOURCE
16192 Coastal Highway
Lewes, DE 19958. U.S.A.

Table of Content

SUMMARY 1

SPORADES ISLANDS GREECE.. 4
- INTRODUCTION 4
- THE HISTORY 5
- SPORADES ISLANDS: ISLANDS TRAVEL GUIDE 10
  - *Alonissos Island* 10
    - Patitiri 14
    - The Old Town (Hora) 18
    - History of Alonissos 21
    - Beaches of Alonissos 23
    - Marine Park & Daily Excursions 25
    - Where to Stay 27
      - Milia Bay Hotel and Apartments 28
      - Pension Nina 30
      - Yalis Hotel 30
      - Pension Votsi 31
      - Angelos Apartments 32
      - Old Village 32
      - Ikion Eco Boutique Hotel 33
      - Alonissos Beach Bungalows And Suites Hotel 34
      - Elma's Houses 35
    - Where To Eat 37
    - Art, Artists and Healers 40
  - *Skiathos Island* 43
    - History of Skiathos 45
      - Prehistoric times (-1100 B.C.) 45
      - Early and Classical times (1100-338 B.C.) 46
      - Hellenistic and Roman times (338 B.C. - 330 A.D.) ... 51
      - The Byzantine period and Venetian rule (330-1538 A.D.) 53
      - The Greek War of Independence (1821) 59
    - Skiathos Excursions and Touring 61
    - Skiathos Cities and Towns 66
      - Kanapitsa Beach 66
        - Kanapitsa Holidays Excursions 68
        - Things To See 70

- Koukounaries 72
- Megali Amos 74
- Skiathos Town 78

Skopelos Island *83*
- Skopelos History 86
- Island's Culture 92
- Events 96
  - Skopelos Film Festival... 97
  - Glossa Festival 98
  - Rembetiko festival 99
  - Skopelian Week 99
- Skopelos: Excursions and Touring...................................... 100
- Skopelos Town 103
- Skopelos Tourist Guide 106
  - Hóra And Around... 109
  - Alphonse The Philhellene Spy....................................... 113
  - South & West Coast Beaches Of Skopelos.................... 115
  - Far Northwest Skopelos 116
  - Recommended Walking Maps And Guides 119
  - Skopelos Accommodation 120
  - Getting To And Around Skopelos 126

Skyros Island *128*
- History of Skyros 130
  - Prehistoric Era 131
  - Mythical evidence 133
  - Historical Times 138
  - Byzantine Times... 139
  - Medieval Times 141
  - Turkish Rule 146
  - Modern Times 152
- Skyros Cities and Towns... 153
  - Gyrismata 153
  - Magazia 154
  - Skyros Town 156

Summary

Sporades Islands Greece Guide: It is regretting that certain people have a mindset that traveling is a waste of time, energy and money. Some also find traveling an extremely boring activity.

Nevertheless, a good majority of people across the world prefer traveling, rather than staying inside the confined spaces of their homes. They love to explore new places, meet new people, and see things that they would not find in their homelands. It is this very popular attitude that has made tourism, one of the most profitable, commercial sectors in the world.

People travel for various reasons. Some travel for work, others for fun, and some for finding mental peace. Though every person may have his/her own reason to go on a journey, it is essential to note that traveling, in itself, has some inherent advantages. For one, for some days getting away from everyday routine is a pleasant change. It not only refreshes one's body, but also mind and soul. Traveling to a distant place and doing exciting things that are not thought of otherwise, can rejuvenate a person, who then returns home, ready to take on new and more difficult challenges in life and work. It makes a person forget his worries, problems, frustrations, and fears, albeit for some time. It gives him a chance to think wisely and constructively. Traveling also helps to heal; it can mend a broken heart.

For many people, traveling is a way to attain knowledge, and perhaps, a quest to find answers to their questions. For this, many people prefer to go to faraway and isolated places. For believers, it is a search for God and to gain higher knowledge; for others, it is a search for inner peace. They might or might not find what they are looking for, but such an experience certainly enriches their lives.

Celebrating: There's always a happy reason to take a trip. It could be a landmark birthday or anniversary. A graduation. A wedding or pre-wedding festivities. Even a babymoon before a little one arrives. A special occasion is made even more special by celebrating away from the hectic pace of life at home. It's also a good way to gather family and friends from distant corners to mark the milestone. Celebration vacations provide a lasting benefit as well: shared memories for a lifetime.

Sporades Islands Greece..
Introduction

The group of Sporades islands is located off Mount Pelion, in the northwestern Aegean Sea. It actually consists of four Greek islands (Skiathos, Skopelos, Alonissos, and Skyros) and few uninhabited islets that form the Marine Park of North Aegean Sea.

The most popular island of Sporades is Skiathos, famous for the lovely sandy beaches and the intense nightlife. Skopelos and Alonissos are less popular beaches, but they amaze visitors with the green landscape and the relaxing coves. Skiathos and Skopelos were also the islands where scenes for the Hollywood movie Mamma Mia (2008) were shot.

Skyros is the least famous island of the group, mostly due to its distance from the rest Sporades and the sparse transportation. It is a beautiful place for relaxing, family vacations away from large crowds. According to mythology, Skyros was the island where king Theseus was assassinated and also where Achilles went to hide to avoid the Trojan War. Eventually, Ulysses and few other Greeks found him and convinced him to participate in the expedition.

The History

Sporades are one of the lesser-known and least-visited island groups in the Mediterranean. Remarkably verdant, only a few are inhabited, including Skiathos, Skopelos and Alonisso. They all host a wide range of beautiful beaches lapped by stunningly blue waters along with pine-fragrant hills that make this archipelago an ideal destination for nature lovers. Sporades Islands Overview While the Sporades archipelago can be reached by ferry from Agios Constantinos a couple hours north of Athens, many travelers fly into the international airport on the island of Skiathos. Sometimes referred to as the "Mykonos of the Sporades," this island offers the most in terms of touristic facilities, including lots of nightlife options. It's also home to some of the best beaches in Greece, with over 60 beaches along a 27-mile coastline. There are options for relaxing in secluded coves as well as beaches for enjoying water sports and lively stretches for partying. Skiathos town is filled with restaurants, bars, unique shops and luxury hotels, and boasts traditional architecture, including small whitewashed homes and red tiled roofs that makes it look like a postcard.

Skopelos is a nature lover's paradise with forests, spectacular coastline and a variety of wildlife, including monk seals. It has multiple archaeological sites, monasteries and some 360 churches along with good nightlife options and fantastic dining. It was also the main filming location for "Mamma Mia!" Alonissos is popular with travelers seeking solitude, far away from the tourist crowds. It's blessed with rugged natural landscapes, pine forests, olive groves and beautiful beaches with crystal-clear blue waters, as well as being home to the National Marine Park of Northern Sporades, a refuge for the Mediterranean monk seal, dolphins and rare sea birds. Sporades Islands History in a Nutshell Archaeological evidence has revealed that the Sporades have been inhabited from the Palaeolithic period. For several centuries, the

Sporades were part of the great Minoan empire. After the mysterious demise of the civilization, the archipelago was dominated by the Mycenaeans. During both these periods, the islands flourished thanks to commercial domination which was at the root of the Minoans and Mycenaeans success.

Sporades was an ally with the Athenians during classical antiquity. In 478 BC Skiathos joined forces with the Athenians in the struggle against Persia, subsequently becoming part of the Athenian Alliance, enjoying a period of independence until the archipelago succumbed to Philip II of Macedonia and his son, Alexander the Great followed by the Romans in the 2nd century BC. After the fall of the Roman Empire, the Sporades suffered from many pirate invasions and were used as places of exile as the unfrequented backwaters of the Byzantine Empire. The islands fell under Venetian occupation in the 13th century, incorporated as part of the trade route for the Maritime Republic of Venice. They thrived due to the commercial traffic that passed through.

After centuries of relative peace, the Ottomans attacked in 1583, destroying villages and slaughtering inhabitants. The archipelago was virtually uninhabited for a generation before being liberated from the Ottomans and the Treaty of Constantinople of 1832. With Greece recognized as a sovereign nation, the Sporades were incorporated into the new Greek State. The islands were relatively unaffected by World War II although Skiathos Town was badly bombed. The earthquake of 1965 caused significant damage to old Alonissos Town which was abandoned residents moved to the new town of Patitiri further down the coast.

Sporades Islands: Islands Travel Guide

Alonissos Island

The main island of Alonissos forms part of the National Marine Park, where many of the smaller surrounding islands are under the full protection of the government in order to protect a variety of species, from rare plants to falcons, gulls and other birds, as well as the monk seal and a species of wild goat. In fact, Alonissos is the only inhabited island of the full cluster of nine smaller islands and islets, five of which are strictly protected by environmental laws, and one of which is totally off-limits to visitors.

Alonissos, lying approximately 62 nautical miles from Volos on the mainland, and with a year-round population of about 2,000 inhabitants, is fairly well developed for tourism, especially in its southern portion and along the east coast. A paved road connects the main towns on the east coast (Patitiri, the harbor, main town, and current capital and beautiful Votsi, just north of the harbor) with the old capital, called Chora or Old Alonissos, situated high on the hillside and just inland from the east coast.

From Patitiri, there is a lovely path that you can walk the three kilometers uphill to reach the old capital. Regular bus service runs between the two, and caiques from Patitiri can take you to numerous beaches on the east coast, as well as to some of the protected islands of the park to the north and northeast of Alonissos.

Further north along the east coast is the charming natural harbor and village of Steni Vala, offering tavernas in a lovely setting and with superb views. Here is a Rescue Center for the monk seals, primarily treating wounded and orphaned pups. Moving further north along a newly paved road, you'll arrive at Geraka Bay, which is home to a Biological Station observing and monitoring the ecosystem and, particularly, the monk seal.

There are some lovely beaches on both the east and west coasts of the island. Of notable mention are Milia, Kokkinokastro, Gerakas, Mourtias, and Ai. Dimitrios. As the island is mostly pine covered, you will continually see the striking contrast between the intense green of the island and the deep blue of the sea.

The most developed village of the island is the present capital, Patitiri. It is here that you'll find accommodation, tourist services, banking, supermarkets, the health center, and the police. There is an ample selection of tavernas and restaurants, shopping, and even a bit of nightlife.

This village was developed after 1965, when most of the inhabitants fled the old capital after a destructive earthquake destroyed much of the hilltop village. While the architecture of the buildings of Patitiri is not nearly as attractive as that of the old capital, the setting around the natural port with its small marina is absolutely lovely.

UNLIKE the other islands in the Sporades group Skiathos, Skyros and Skopelos - Alonissos is not often expounded on in travel guides or even glossy conversations about the Greek islands. Sailing into the Alonissos harbor you instantly sense the singular atmosphere, non-pretentious elegance and relaxing appeal of this island. The colors of the sea, sky, pine and olive trees tumbling into waters, and the architectural style, immediately present a special, more individual character. Upon stepping onto the port of Patitiri, every encounter with the sociable locals only proves that here the people are surprisingly genuine, down-to-earth and tranquil, seemingly unaffected by the tourism-oriented country's prime drive to simply make money from you.

In Alonissos one really feels they are experiencing the exquisiteness, innocence and unassuming charm of how Greek islands were before the mass tourism boom, when eating fresh fish, sipping iced ouzo at twilight and listening to Syrtaki was not yet burdensomely clichéd. In fact, practically everywhere we visited we heard old bouzouki classics piping through the speakers rather than the usual dance / lounge / pop / rock songs, and although this did sound a bit cheesy it was actually also very sweet to be unassumingly transported through time.

Patitiri

The port town of Patitiri is the island's most lively spot, but even so, manages to retain a sense of simple fun rather than turning into a mad, crowded people-watching orgy. Upon arriving at the port we opted for a refreshing glass of chilled white wine at Aesop's Cave, a café / bar with a shockingly tacky but (to be fair) original exterior where the service was so accommodating and the prices so reasonable that it became our main hangout whenever we swung that way. The café is an ideal place to meet locals and expats who have settled on the island, such as Thomas and Belinda from England who related to us how they fell in love with Alonissos when there on an accidental visit and have now retired there, enjoying long walks along the island's many (there are around 14 in total) pathways and being part of friendly Greek-foreign community. The port is lined with cafes and tavernas, and further towards the right becomes quite cosy with a small strip of smaller eateries and bars, which at night are wonderful to sit in as they face the sea and are right beside a large, limestone rock facade lit up in a soft green light.

At the port you'll find all your essentials foreign and Greek press, the island's one and only internet café, beach and swimming gear (including fishing guns, flippers, snorkels), some trendy clothes shops and the usual tourist trinkets. The tourist offices there offer a variety of day-trips to the Marine Park (we favoured Ikos Travel Tour with the legendary Captain Pikos, whose enthralling tales about the island's history, mythology and culture are not to be missed) and other destinations, and there are also several car / bike rental places.

Once there, it's also well worth visiting the Women's Association of Alonissos, where the 15 or so women sell homemade sweets, pickled tuna, olives as well as fresh herb, spinach and cheese pies, and pasta all of which are made from traditional recipes passed on through the generations. The Association opened in 2000 and welcomes customers year-round throughout the day, aiming to keep the island's food culture alive. We were surprised to not see more use of the island's overabundance of herbs as Alonissos is renowned throughout Greece for its plethora of herbs, as they only had the usual dried sage, mountain tea, oregano, thyme and chamomile, but we found out that since the '70s the island's main industry is tourism and fishing, and that "no one can find the time to cultivate and pick herbs". The prices at the Women's Association shop are reasonable, with herb-smoked pickled local tuna at

10 euros for a large jar and traditional wedding and celebration almond and flower-water (amygdalota) sweets or walnut and honey (bourekia) sweets sold by the piece.

The Old Town (Hora)

Hawks, rare passion flowers, butterflies, honeysuckle and ripe apricots make up only a part of the vibrant paradise-like environment of the old town and the island overall. In our first day in the Chora we came across an adder scuttling across the pathway and instead of feeling alarmed we were pleased to be surrounded by real, living nature, going about its own life rather than being in an environment solely controlled by man.

Even if you choose not to stay there, the Old Town is a must-see place, but try and avoid it between 11-1pm when bus-loads of tourists on cruises take over. Enjoy a leisurely ouzo or coffee at Haiati with its dramatic views of the valleys and sea. The café-restaurant, which also offers live music at night, is owned by a lady from Thessaloniki whose family originated from Capadocia in Eastern Turkey, and as both those places are known for their spell-binding cuisine it's no surprise that her food holds secret treasures from her roots (it is said that Capadocia is the place of origin for tortellini a fact hotly disputed by the Italians) but trying the cheese and herb pitta or the minced meat pie, topped with yogurt or spicy red sauce made according to her grandmothers recipes it is easy to see why (you can order these and have them made there and then, but be prepared to wait 20 minutes).

Strolling through the Old Town is a mesmerising experience because of its distinct traditional style, with cobblestone streets, stone stairways sharply leading you into veiled pockets where you'll discover small, long-established stores with homemade food products or wines and hand-picked medicinal herbs. Take in the Venentian-inspired golden and rust-coloured architecture and above all, a sense of calm, easy living, where, as locals will tell you, a sense of innocence and trust pervades. Within one day of staying there we were on first-name basis with various shop-owners and taverna waiters, and our second favourite café, Aerides, set in a shady, green-filled little square and decked out with wooden benches, tables and chairs, had no qualms to lend us their backgammon set for a couple of days. The nightlife is more on the quiet side, but you can head to the newly opened Sofrano bar near the main square, where you can stay long enough to soak in the awe-inspiring sight of sunrise over the sea and mountains.

In the Chora you will find two mini-markets and several tourist shops selling toys modelled on the Monachus Monachus seal and on dolphins, T-shirts themed on the marine park and traditional food, cosmetic products and trinkets.

History of Alonissos

History maintains that the Cretans, led by the legendary hero Staphylos, established colonies on Alonissos (then known as Ikos) during the Minoan domination of the Aegean Sea, circa the 16th century B.C. The Minoan colony, which later became Mycenean, stood on the site today known as Kokkinokastro. History says that the Geometric period finds Ikos under the domination of the Dolopes, who emerged eventually as a pirate group that terrorized the Aegean, until the Athenian navy crushed their force under the leadership of Kimon, who in 476 B.C. annexed Ikos to the first Athenian Alliance.

During the classical period Ikos is said to have been made up of two cities, Kokkinokastro, where ruins of a fortified wall remain today, and the village of Old Alonissos. During this period the island was renowned for its vineyards and its exceptional wine. In 190 B.C. Ikos was occupied by the Roman navy, and, the next period documented historically, fell into the hands of the Venetian Ghisi family in 1207, after which it was occupied by the Turks in 1538 under the control of the savage pirate Khair-ed-Din Barbarossa, who is said to have slaughtered the entire population of the Old Town. The Turkish domination continued until 1830 when Alonissos became part of the new and free Hellenic State, together with the rest of the Sporades Islands.

Beaches of Alonissos

The Island's beaches are generally characterized by their exceptionally clean, cool, crystal waters, most of which are a sparkling emerald or turquoise colour. Every beach we visited, however, has its own distinctive character. Here is a listing of our top 5:

Megalos Mourtias: Lounging on the foothill below the Old Town in the neighbouring gulf, this beach has flat stones and is flanked by rocky walls. As with most beaches on Alonissos there isn't a mass of chaise longue and beach umbrellas taking over the beach, but there are a few straw umbrellas and chairs and there is a patch of olive groves behind the beach where you can take a snooze. We had lunch at the prettily decorated Meltemi, surprisingly it was rated by Athinorama magazine's gastronomic supplement as serving the best lobster pasta.

Milia: This long bay emerges after a small trek through a thick pine-forest and has both sand and stones. The sandy sea-bed feels crunchy when you step on it and you might smell something that reminds you a little of sulphur, which locals offer various renditions to explain: some say it is indeed beneficial sulphur, while others say it's the black seaweed growing in the sea bed, is considered to be very rejuvenating for the skin and even able to treat cellulite. The beach has no umbrellas or bar but its crystal clear waters offer a refreshing respite from the summer heat.

Kokkinokastro: The deep blue sea, imposingly tall red rocks, yellow sand, pine trees and colourful pebbles make this ancient settlement one of the most impressive beaches on the island. On this reasonably large beach you can also rent out a pedalo or canoe for some beach action.

Yialia: This tiny cove is characterized by the windmill that stands on its left-hand edge and pebbles in different shades of grey. As you enter it suddenly plunges into deep, cool water, and we found it was the perfect beach from where to watch the sun set, while inside the sea.

Tsoukalia: This archaeological site is most unusual as it used to be the home of a pottery factory, and until today the entire beach is scattered with broken bits of pottery from vases and vessels that look new but are actually at least 2000 years old. If you go snorkeling you will also spot large vessels broken into chunks and serving as fish hotels as they sit lodged between rocks. Simmers will also enjoy a little cove off the left hand side of the beach where one can lie on the pebbles in complete privacy after a 15 minute swim.

Marine Park & Daily Excursions

The National Marine Park was founded by Presidential Decree in May 1992 and protects 10 percent of the world's endangered Monachus Monachus seal population, which is one of the largest seal species in the world, with a length of 2-3 metres and an average weight of 250 kg. The Mediterranean monk seal is represented on ancient Greek coins and passages by Homer describe it basking in the sun on sandy beaches. The Alonissos municipality writes that "Today, the largest population of seals in the Mediterranean is found in Greece, spread out over the whole of the Aegean and Ionian Seas, while it is significant that the species has essentially disappeared from the industrialised Western Mediterranean. This makes it easy to appreciate the importance of the Park in protecting the seals. Because of its morphology and position, the Park is an ideal habitat, rich in food. The active participation of the region's fishermen and the fishing Cooperative of Alonissos in the protection effort is significant, and has largely contributed to the elimination of the deliberate killing of seals in the area of the Park."

Alonissos is the largest island in the Park, which also encompasses six smaller islands (Peristera, Kyra Panagia, Gioura, Skantzoura, and Piperi) and 22 uninhabited islands and rocky outcrops. The day trip includes visits to all these places.

Where to Stay

Alonissos offers a broad choice of accommodations around the island: rooms-to-let (you can find the Association of Rooms-to-let Owners at the port) and studios or apartments, especially in Patitiri, the Old Town, Rouroum-Yialo, Votsi, Steni-Vala, Milia and Kalamakia. You can also find quality A to C class hotels and bungalows, as well as two camping sites, at Steni-Vala and Plakes near the harbour. The latter campsite, called 'Camping Rocks' had come highly recommended by nature-loving friends, as it is set in 13 stremmata of pine forest only 50 meters from the beach of plakes, (flat rocks). It has W.C. and shower facilities, a kitchen area with a grill and sinks while, from next summer ('08) it will also open a cafeteria serving breakfast and snacks. Upon visiting the site we spoke with owner Giorgos Agalou who was sweatily busy renovating it for the high season. There was no one staying there at the time and although such circumstances can be ideal for some we opted to stay in the peacefully serene Milia Bay and later the wonderfully picturesque Chora instead.

Milia Bay Hotel and Apartments

Milia Bay Hotel and Apartments, with its breathtaking views of Milia Bay and the Aegean archipelago, is set in a lush, whispering landscape and offers sunny studios as well as one and two bedroom apartments decorated with traditional and antique furniture. Its overall style and décor reflect its owners, the Meyanas family, who are low-key, graceful and friendly individuals with a long experience in hospitality and a great connection to every aspect of life on Alonissos. You can enjoy tasty, homemade-style breakfast, lunch or dinner at the Sifandas restaurant veranda by the pool, overlooking the serene seascapes, or even choose to cook your own dinner in the summer villa-like ambience of your own apartment, since each accommodation is supplied with a kitchenette, (all cooking materials and fridge included). Andreas, who runs the hotel with his Belgian mother and sister, is also the Tourism Director for the Alonissos Municipality, and will generously offer you any kind of advice and information on what to see and do. In our first encounter he offered us a hand-painted map of the island and instantly got on the phone to help us book a brand new jeep for a bargain price. Everyone we met on the island had only the best things to say about the family and the scenic hotel. Another plus is that Milia Bay is only 10 minutes walk from Milia beach (see beaches).

Pension Nina

Pension Nina is 2 minutes walk from the beach and overlooks the port of Patitiri, with its cafes and tavernas. It features traditionally styled rooms with free Wi-Fi and views of the sea. Pension Ninna's colourful rooms include handmade iron beds, a TV and refrigerator. Each is air conditioned and has a private bathroom with hairdryer. Apartments and studios with kitchenettes are available.

Yalis Hotel

Located in Vótsi, Yalis Hotel features a seasonal outdoor pool and sun terrace. Guests can enjoy the on-site restaurant. Free WiFi is featured throughout the property and free private parking is available on site. Each room has a flat-screen TV. Certain units have a sitting area where you can relax. Certain rooms include views of the sea or garden. Each room is fitted with a private bathroom.

Pension Votsi
Located in Vótsi, just a 2 minute walk from the beach, Pension Votsi features free WiFi, a garden and sun terrace. The property is air conditioned and features a satellite flat-screen TV. A refrigerator and coffee machine are also featured. There is also a kitchenette in some of the units equipped with an oven and stovetop. Every unit is fitted with a private bathroom with free toiletries and a hairdryer. Bed linen are provided.

Angelos Apartments

Showcasing a sun terrace and views of the sea, Angelos Apartments is located in Patitírion a one minute walk from the beach. Featuring a balcony, the accommodation has a dining area and a sitting area with a cable TV. There is also a kitchen in some of the units equipped with a refrigerator. There is a private bathroom with a shower and slippers in each unit.

Old Village

Old Village is in the village of Alonnisos. With interior stone finishes and wood beam ceilings, the 2-story villas feature free Wi-Fi and a furnished balcony with mountain and Mediterranean Sea views. Modernly decorated, the units include an open-plan living, dining and functional kitchen area with a ceramic top stove. Each features a fireplace, flat-screen satellite TV and CD player. They include 2 bedrooms and air conditioning. Old Village provides private parking on site. The main port of Patitiri, traditional taverns, cafe-bars and shops are all 2 miles away.

Ikion Eco Boutique Hotel

This fully renovated green hotel in Patitiri, is only 500 feet from Roussoum Gialos beach. It features a spacious breakfast lounge and luxurious rooms with free Wi-Fi. Ikion Eco Boutique Hotel is comprised of bright and airy rooms with furnished balconies with view of the sea or the mountain. Family rooms are also available. All units are air-conditioned and feature a multitude of amenities including anatomic mattresses and pillows. A healthy breakfast, prepared with local ingredients and enriched with homemade Greek flavors, is served daily at the dining area. Restaurants and mini markets can be found within a short walk of the property. The bus stop and shopping area are just 300 feet away. The port is just over a quarter mile from the Ikion Hotel. The front desk is open 24 hours, offering information on car rental, excursions, tours, activities, ticket reservations and more.

Alonissos Beach Bungalows And Suites Hotel

Right on its private beach area of Chrisi Milia, the 4-star Alonissos Beach features elegant accommodation, an outdoor pool and tennis court, amidst lush greenery. Dining options include a rooftop restaurant, poolside bar and snack bar. Fitted with light wood furnishings, all air-conditioned rooms and suites open to a balcony, some with Aegean Sea view. Each has a satellite TV, mini fridge and free toiletries. Some also offer a private pool or outdoor hot tub. Guests at Alonissos Beach Bungalows And Suites Hotel can start their day with a buffet breakfast. Greek and Italian dishes, enriched with local specialties are served at the on-site restaurant. Enjoying sea views, the 2 bars prepare snacks and cocktails. Sport facilities include a 5x5 soccer field, well-equipped gym and games room with billiards and table tennis. Guests can spoil themselves with a massage treatment, steam bath or sauna. Free Wi-Fi is available in the reception.

Elma's Houses

alonissos, greeceWishing to experience various aspects of the island, we chose to also stay in the quaint Chora (the Old Town of Alonissos). During a visit to the shop Gorgona, a three-storey antique shop showcasing a great deal of the island's but also the country's culture and tradition, we discovered that its owner Elma, who is an architect and photographer (you'll find postcards with her pictures in various spots around the island) had just finished renovating three traditional houses designed to accommodate eclectic vacationers. Elma's Houses, located on the hillside of the Old

Town and reachable via a short walk down characteristic lovely cobblestone steps heading towards the Old School, were exactly what we wished for before knowing they existed.

With support from the European Union and the Greek National Tourism Organisation, Elma fully renovated the houses (joined by a pretty courtyard and overlooking the sea) following strict guidelines to not disrupt or change any element of their traditional style. The result is fully self-sufficient accommodations suited to modern needs with unique island old-style charm such as the raised bed, the fireplace decorated by hand-painted plates, and the ceiling-door that separates the downstairs from the kitchen and sitting room upstairs. We relished sipping our Greek coffee and eating fresh bread slathered in apricot jam made by Elma's husband on our little balcony overlooking the sea, red ceramic tiled rooftops and trees while staying in the Blue House.

Where To Eat

There is no doubt in the Alonissian universe that 'Tassia's Cooking' in the lovely, tiny fishing village of Steni Vala serves the most scrumptious food. In our 10-day stay on the island we went there three times, and it is really one of those places that you know you'll dream nostalgically about after you leave. Head to Steni Vala just after sunset and as you approach along the curvy road, stop to get a birds eye view of the fairy-tale like village: the glittering sea, dim lights and thick greenery where fishing and sail boats huddle together in the marina. At Steni Vala, where one can also find accommodation, there are another two tavernas and a café. We hit the culinary jackpot by following the travelers wisdom that you should opt for the restaurant where you see the most locals, although many foreigners step off their sail-boats to enjoy the restaurant's fresh seafood and fish dishes, creamy feta cheese, crunchy salads such as the very rarely found kritamo, which usually requires acrobatic skills to pick as it grows on the craggy edges of rocks towering over the sea and feeds chiefly off the salt and iodine rich sea air.

Although lobster is the island's trademark seafood, for us the main attraction was Tassia's amazing crayfish pasta (karavido-makaronada) which even by Alexia's raised-in-Italy standards was cooked to perfection and exactly as teasingly spicy as we indulgently requested. We did also try the lobster pasta (a Greek obsession and never below a biting 60 euros in price on islands & mainland alike) and although tasty it paled in comparison. The service at Tassia's is very friendly, with waitresses comfortably chatting to us about their careers in athletics and a maitre'd / sports trainer, and the décor is perfectly cosy, with the large veranda bedecked by a multitude of robust local plants like gardenia, jasmine and basil, the smells from which waft through the air as you smile into your hima wine.

In contrast, Kalamakia, the island's other small fishing village, was a disappointment. Although aesthetically this too is attractive enough, with its marina full of local fishing boats and tavernas named after the sea hunters, the taveras here were so obviously geared at tourists, and the service and food so average, that there was simply not enough magic to tie in with the rest of the island. Plastic signs advertising food in English are set outside each place and the lighting is neon striped, something which we frankly will only tolerate in the Athinas meat-market in central Athens at 5am.

Art, Artists and Healers

Bente Keller & Ilias Tsoukanas: are hot stuff on the island, and you will inevitably hear about them during your visit or spot one of their two comprehensively researched and colourfully informative books, 'Alonissos on Foot' and 'The Alonissos Guide' at some point. The Danish-Greek duo (Bente arrived on the island 20 years ago and eventually married Ilias, a former fisherman) are youthful and energetic. They have intimate knowledge and understanding of the island which they express in their books. These are filled with Bente's landscape watercolours depicting Alonissos. You can visit them at 'gallery 5' in the Old Town. There you will find original artworks, prints, homemade candles and ceramic art from the Sporades islands.

Professor George Vithoulkas at the Academy of Homeopathy: In Alonissos you can find The

International Academy of Classical Homeopathy (I.A.C.H.), directed by Professor George Vithoulkas. Doctors from around the world flock to the island for his seminars courses, and locals speak of him with awe. Even though he is extremely busy, his very capable and organised staff will show you around and advise you on any books of his you might be interested in buying.

Bibi and Lee Hamblin have just built their house / yoga studio / therapy space called Kali Thea (Fine View) on Alonissos where they moved to from London. The dynamic and charismatic couple offer a series of alternative therapies such as hot stone, Swedish, Thai and reflexology massage as well as 1-week-long Ashtanga and Hatha yoga classes catering to groups or individuals. Both Lee, who used to work as a song writer and music producer at Island Records and practices Ashtanga at least two hours per day, and Bibi, who met Lee at the same workplace in 1989 and in her gradual attraction towards healing went to London's College of Psychic Studies, are both highly qualified and fully live their art. We tried the Thai and Swedish massages, which had profound energising and relaxing effects respectively, and enjoyed speaking with them about their new life adventure on the island.

Scottish-born John Simpson settled in Alonissos seven years ago, having fallen head over heels with the island and feeling he was answering a calling to create art there. With a background in social services in England and dairy farming (as well as learning and successfully practicing Bioenergetic Farming) in New Zealand, the youthful, spiritual and charming Simpson has become quite a legend on the island, where his art is exhibited in the museum. Find out more about the sculptor and his work directly at: +30 6972 127 405

Skiathos Island

In the Sporades group, Skiathos is the smallest in size, yet has the largest tourist infrastructure, and attracts the largest number of visitors to this part of the Aegean. It is also the nearest to the mainland, and probably the easiest to reach, whether by ferry or by plane.

There is no question that this lovely island deserves the attention that it gets. Its beaches are legendary, its lifestyle is quite cosmopolitan, and it boasts of a lovely capital, and many pretty resort-style settlements along its magnificent shores. It's a bit like encountering Mykonos, but with trees and red-roofed houses! And, like Mykonos, Skiathos has an enormous amount of charm and outstanding beaches, though it is half the size of its Cycladic counterpart.

Skiathos is situated only 40 nautical miles east of Volos on the mainland and is reached by ferry from both Volos and Ai. Konstantinos, and with less frequent service from Thessaloniki in the north, and Evia in the south. It also connects frequently with the nearby islands of Skopelos and Alonissos. During the summer, there are frequent flights to and from Athens.

The island encompasses approximately 48 square kilometers of pine-covered low hills, with a main road running in a southerly direction from the east coast all the way around to the west coast, to about midpoint on the island. This is where you'll find the best beaches (and there are many!!), with the north coast being accessible only on foot or by caique.

Skiathos is not an island with inland villages; it has the main town and capital, Chora, and lots of little seaside settlements that have been developed for tourism. The year round population totals about 4,000 inhabitants, who live primarily in the capital and occupy themselves with tourism and a bit of fishing.

History of Skiathos

Prehistoric times (-1100 B.C.)

Our earliest information about the history of Skiathos comes from the "Travels"of an anonymous writer, previously thought to have been the geographer Skymnos of Chios. According to the writer of "Travels" then, the island was inhabited in prehistoric times by the Pelasgians, a pre-hellenic tribe which came down from Thrace. It is possible, though, that before the Pelasgian settlement in Skiathos, the island may have been inhabited by Careans who, as the historian

Thucydides tells us, settled in many Greek islands during those times.

However, it is likely that the island was inhabited by other peoples, too, after the Pelasgian settlement. Amongst these, for instance, there may have been Cretans who, we know, had occupied neighbouring Peparithos (or Skopelos, as it is called today). This hypothesis is supported by the fact that one of the names by which the god Dionysos was called in the islands occupied by the Cretans was "Skiathos" - an adjective which bears a very close resemblance to the name of the island. Finally, it is also probable that Thessalians, of the Mycenean age, had settled on Skiathos.

Early and Classical times (1100-338 B.C.)

After these ancient settlers, the islands were inhabited by the Chalcedeans. These were Ionians who came to Skiathos during the period of their colonizing activities from the 8th century on. They seem to have arrived on the island during the 7th or 6th century, on their way to found colonies in Chalcidice (Macedonia). They built their town on the southeastern side of the harbour, on a height, where it could command a view and control the large bay and the inner double harbour. The town was encircled by a wall of square marble blocks, large and rough-hewn, and two gates assured communication with the hinterl and and the harbour. This town survived all through the Classical, Hellenistic and Byzantine periods, until the time when the medieval town, the Kastro (fortress) was built on the northern side of the island.

Skiathos reappears on the historical scene during the Persian wars. As the historian Herodotus tells us, in 480 B.C.,when the Persian fleet was sailing down from Thessaloniki, the Greeks awaiting it at

Artemision in Euboea, were warned by lighted torches on Skiathos. It seems that, during this period, Skiathos helped the Greeks and was perhaps one of the few cities which did not go over to the Medes. When the 1st Athenian Alliance - known as the Delian Alliance was founded in 478/7, Skiathos took the side of the Athenians. Allied towns were divided into regions for tax-collecting purposes and from the "taxation lists", still pre-served in attic inscriptions, we can see that Skiathos was included in the Thracian region and paid 1.000 drachmae a year - a very small sum, which indicates that Skiathos was poor at the time. During the period of the Athenian Alliance, Skiathos had its own democratic and autonomous administration, as did the other allied cities. That is, it had its own Boule (administrative/legislative council, its citizens' assembly ("ecclesia"), and an eponymous archon (member of the executive in office for a year,and whose name was used to designate that year). In the end, however, the alliance developed into an hegemony with the Athenians exercising dominance over their allies and an authoritarian form of goverment.

At the end of the Peloponnesian war in 404 B.C., when the Athenians were defeated by the Spartans, Skiathos came under the rule of Sparta and her system of goverment became that of an oligarchy. In 386 B.C. during the Antalcidean or Basilean peace, in accordance with which all the islands with the exception of Limnos, Imbros and Skyros where the Athenians allotted holdings to settlers - were granted their autonomy,Skiathos, too, was officially declared independent. The Spartans, however, violated the peace treaty and soon seized Skiathos again, together with other islands,where they left a garrison and imposed heavy taxes.

In 378/7 B.C., Athens established the 2nd Athenian Alliance, a genuinely defensive alliance this time, with the aim of opposing the expansionist intentions of the Spartans. Skiathos once again ranged itself with Athens, following the campaign of general Chabrias in Euboea and the Northern Sporades in 377 B.C. Skiathos remained in the 2nd Athenian Alliance with its autonomy and democratic institutions, approximately 40 years. And it seems that during this period, the island's financial situation improved so much that it was able, towards the middle of the 4th century B.C., to mint bronze coins with the head of Hermes on one side and his caduceus (staff) with the word CKIAΘI in the other. Later, the island was used by the Athenians as a naval port and a base for its expeditions against Philip II of Macedonia.

In 338 B.C., after the battle of Chaeronea, which virtually brought to an end the independence of the southern Greekstates and marked the beginning ofMacedonian domination, Skiathos came under Macedonian rule .

Hellenistic and Roman times (338 B.C. - 330 A.D.)

The Macedonians established an oligarchic system of government in Skiathos and the island remained undisturbed for , many years. Historically, it emerges again from the time of Philip V (238-279 B.C.), the Macedonian king who was, at that time, at war with the Romans. This was a troubled period for the island, as the surrounding areas became scenes of battle. When the 2nd Macedonian war began, in 200/199 B.C., Philip ordered Skiathos and Skopelos to be destroyed to prevent their falling into the hands of the enemy fleet and being used against him. And indeed, in the same year, the Roman fleet, together with that of Attalus I of Pergamum, who was an ally of Rome, arrived on the island, and plundered whatever was left after Philip's raid. Despite the great extent of the destruction, the town quickly recovered and, following Philip's defeat at Kynos Kephales in 197 B.C., democracy was again restored. When the Macedonian Kingdom was overthrown in 168 B.C., the Romans granted a degree of freedom to the Greek cities and states.

Finally, however in 146 B.C., the whole of Greece was subjugated by the Romans and Skiathos followed the fate of the rest of the country. In 42 B.C., after the battle of Philippi the victor, Antony, handed over Skiathos along with some other islands to the Athenians, as a token of gratitude for their friendly attitude towards him. Skiathos thus re-established its democratic regime, along with the Athenians, and retained it well into the years following the birth of Christ.

The Byzantine period and Venetian rule (330-1538 A.D.)

The information we have on Shiathos during the first years of the Byzantine period is extremely scanty. All we know is that, administratively, it belonged to the province of Thessaly, which constituted part of a Macedonian "theme" (military district) and that, with the propagation of Christianity on the island, an episcopate (bishopric) was created under the Metropolitan Bishop of Larissa. In 758 A.d., during the reign of Constantine Copronymus, the Byzantine fleet anchored in Skiathos harbour, whence it sped to the rescue of Thessalonica, where a Bulgarian and Slav attack was imminent . During the 7th century A.D., Skiathos suffered much from Saracen pirate raids in the Aegean.

Following the overthrow of the Byzantine Empire by the Franks, in 1204, and concession of the

Aegean islands to the Venetians, Skiathos, Skopelos and islands of the Cyclades were taken over by the brothers Andrea and Jeremia Ghisi, Venetian merchants. The Ghisi brothers granted Skiathos self-deterrnination, and several privileges, which are listed in the well-known "Capitula Sciati et Scopuli", and which were still in effect during the 2nd period of Venetian rule. However, they abolished the Orthodox episcopate. They built a new fortress called Bourtzi in the great harbour for their residence and for the security of the town.

The Ghisi brothers ruled the islands until 1259, their successors continuing for a further 17 years, until 1276, when the Byzantine fleet drove them out of the N. Sporades. Skiathos remained within the Byzantine state until 1453. Byzantine rule, however, was rather nominal, as the pirate raids that plagued the Aegean at that time did not allow Constantinople to make its presence effectively felt on the islands which it had reclaimed. It thus appears that around the middle of the 14th century, the people of Skiathos, desperate following the continous raids on the island, both of pirates and of Turks, abandoned their coastal town and built a new, safer one - the Kastro ("fortress',) on the northern side of the island, on a steep rock which constituted a naturat fortress.

When Constantinople fell to the Turks in 1453, the people of Skiathos chose Venetian rule, realising that Venice would from then on be their only possible protection against the Turks. They therefore asked the Venetians to take over the island on the condition, however, that they would confirm the privileges that the Ghisi brothers had give the island, and that the see of the Orthodox bishop would remain there, reguests which were granted. Thus began the second period of Venetian rule in Skiathos, which lasted until 1538.

The life of the island, however, did not seem to improuve.

The pirate raids continued and Venetian rules were so harsh, that when, in 1538, the fortress was besieged by Barbarossa, some of the inhabitants, in order to rid themeselves of the tyranny of the Venetians, did not hesitate to surrender it to him. The period of Turkish domination (1538-1821) The Turkish domination of Skiathos began in 1538 officially in 1540 - when the Turco-Venetian peace treaty was signed. During this period the island was ruled by a Turkish governor the voivode, who was assisted by the elders of the town one or two initially, but later more - who were elected each year. Skiathos along with the other islands of the Aegean, belonged to the Kapudan Pacha that is to the admiral of the Turkish fleet.

Each year, the inhabitants paid a certain amount of money as "harach" or tax. There was also a cadi (jude) for legal affairs, an «agha» for administrative affairs and "zambites" who collected the taxes. There were also quite a few Turks living on the island at that time. The inhabitants of Skiathos, as was the case with all the other islanders generally, were requisitioned to serve for a period in the Turkish navy. Later this compulsory service was converted into a contribution in money, the "melachica". However, in the years before the Greek War of Independence, impressment was again brought into effect.

In the mid-17th century, in the year 1660, the Venetian admiral, Francesco Morosini, seized the Kastro and Venetian rule was re-established for the third time. Not for long, however, as the Turks soon took the Kastro again. Thus their domination continued until the beginning of the Greek War of Independence. The Turkish population of Skiathos gradually dwindled. The office of voivode was bought by the locals and there were often no other Turkish officials on the island. Their functions were thus performed by the elders, who gradually acquired more rights. The inhabitants, however continued to suffer pirate raids which still harried them relentlessly. In spite of their trials, the islanders did not lose their interest in navigation.

From the beginning of the 18th century, the people of Skiathos began to build small ships and carry on transportation and commerce with the surrounding areas. Later, on larger ships, they sailed as far as Egypt and the Black Sea. The longing for freedom, however, was still alive in the hearts of the islanders. Thus, in 1770, they took part in the victo- rious sea battle of Chesme, alongside the Russian admiral Alexis

Orlov, and soon afterwards they contributed men and ships to the legendary sea-captain, Lambros Katsonis, who was active against the Turks at the time. In later years (1805-1816) Skiathos effectively helped the chieftains of Mt. Olympus, Giannis Stathas and Nikotsaras, who, after Orlov's revolt had been quashed, continued the fight against the Turks with raids on Turkish shores and attacks on Turkish ships.

An act of great importance both for the island and the whole of Greece was the creation and raising of the first official Greek flag in September 1807, at the holy convent of the Annunciation of the Virgin Mary, in Skiathos.

The Greek War of Independence (1821)

In spite of the fact that it was far from the entre of military operations and thus an easy prey for the Turkish fleet, Skiathos soon joined the ranks of those fighting for Idependence. At that time, it possessed a good number of fully equipped ships, with trained and experienced crews, from the previous sea battles in which they had taken part up until 1816 with the Olympus chieftains. The ships from Skiathos contributed greatly to the War of Independence. At that time many people who had to flee from their homelands when the revoluonary efforts failed, found refuge in Skiathos. An estimated 30,000 refugees from the Pelion villages, from Mt. Olympus, Euboea and Epirus arrived on the island. This influx of population in a restricted space caused problems, as shelter and food became scarce.

Many of the people were armed, and it was not long before fighting broke out and anarchy began to reign. The island was plagued for years by violence and looting, the main offenders being men of Albanian descent ("Liapides") who remained on Skiathos even when most of the refugees had returned to their homelands or settled in safer areas. In 1823 the Turks tried to take the island again but were utterly defeated. In 1829, after the signing of the Protocol of London, on which was based the founding of the Greek state - which, however, remained tributary to the Sultan the inhabitants of Skiathos abandoned the Kastro and resettled along the harbour, where the ancient town had stood.

Skiathos Excursions and Touring

From the capital, there are new roads leading toward the north, which you must combine with walking in order to access the three major inland sites on the island. The old Kastro at the north has the ruins of the old capital and its three remaining churches, plus an outstanding view over the Aegean. There is a path leading down to the windswept pebble beach below. Kastro can also be reached by caique. The monasteries of the island are largely abandoned, but interesting nevertheless. The road north takes you to the inhabited Monastery of Evangelistria, constructed in the late 18th century, the site of the raising of the original blue and white Greek flag in 1827.

From here, you need to travel on foot to reach the abandoned monastery of Ai. Haralambos further north. Toward the northwest, another abandoned monastery, Kechria Monastery, can be reached by a path extending from the main road. This is the oldest monastery on the island, with a path leading down to Kechria beach below (photo to the right). From the new road running from the south to the northwest coast, you can easily reach the pretty monastery called Kounistra, offering a lovely view, excellent icons, and a carved iconostasis.

Exploring the many glorious beaches of Skiathos is easily done by public bus or with car or bike hire. A paved road closely follows the coastline from Chora on the east coast and around the south to Koukounaries on the west coast. To supplement the lack of roads running from beyond Koukounaries and to the north to Kastro, there are many caiques with regular fixed schedules and destinations, all departing from Chora from the secondary port next to Bourtzi. Starting from Chora and working south, the nearest beach is Megali Amos and the resort of Ftelia, which gets quite crowded for its nearness to town; next is Vassilias, followed by Achliadies and Tzaneries, all very busy, well-developed resorts with good beaches. The next major spot is Kanapitsa, which is situated on the Kalamaki peninsula, and offers a wide variety of water sports and a diving center. As you begin to work your way along the southern coast, you will find the lovely beaches of Vromolimnos, Ag. Paraskevi (photo to the left), and Platanias, all excellent beaches with marvelous swimming. The pretty beach of Troullos is perfectly situated opposite some small islets, which add to the charm of its long crescent shape. The connecting road north to the Kounistra Monastery and to the beaches of Aselinos starts from here.

If you continue following this route along the coast, you will next reach one of the most often-photographed beaches of Greece, Koukounaries. This is the last stop on the public bus. You'll find a magnificent beach with a lake positioned behind it, and the sand beach lined with parasol or umbrella pine trees. These imposing trees form a small forest, one of the three such forests existing in Greece, all Ramsar sites and wetlands. This species of pine, with edible seeds, only grow where they have access to brackish water. The lake behind the beach has a narrow tiny canal connecting it to the beach; this is how the lake water gets slightly salinated and suitable for the parasol pine trees, which is what actually Koukounaries means!

Nearby you can walk to the beaches of Krassa (Banana Beach) and Ag. Eleni. You are now on the tiny west coast of the island. After you round the promontory and beyond the pine forest that separates Koukounaries from the north coast, you will arrive to Mandraki (by foot path from Koukounaries). This is another beautiful sand beach backed by high sand dunes, and with a very dramatic presence. Further along is the beach of Elia, fairly quiet and a bit isolated, but with a snack bar. The next two beaches, Megalos Aselinos and Mikros Aselinos can both be reached by the main road to the Kounistra Monastery. Further on, the magnificent beach of Lalaria can only be reached by caique. It is a stunning beach backed and surrounded by perforated white cliffs. The daily caique excursions will explore some inaccessible areas on the north coast, including some of the grottos, particularly the cave of Skotini. This is something that should not be missed!

Skiathos Cities and Towns
Kanapitsa Beach

This small beach is some minutes' walk off the main road and the bus stop. This fact is not necessarily a drawback, since it offers the visitor a tranquil environment. The small beach is well sheltered and placed in a superb pine-tree forest surround. It is seldom crowded and makes a great place to discover. The small taverna on the beach offers fresh fish and salads and local wine; a great place to eat as the sun goes down. The whole beach and its surroundings are just delightful. One can promenade, bicycle or jog along the road going all around the peninsula; fantastic views at every bend and the sounds of local wildlife will make it unforgettable.

Kanapitsa and Tzaneria. Kanapitsa and Tzaneria are two beautiful sandy beaches on the Greek island of Skiathos. They are located a short walk from each other, about eight kilometres from Skiathos Town. Kanapitsa is also the name of the peninsula and the name of the cape here. Following the state road, Kanapitsa and Tzaneria can be reached by exiting from the crossroads.

The road to Kanapitsa goes through a forested hill and descends down to a beautiful sandy beach, with pine trees reaching the sea. On the narrow beach are several terraces where you can have a drink and eat something. The beach is narrow, but has all the amenities; There are sunbeds and umbrellas and you can also do water sports and scuba diving. You can rent a boat and sail around the island. On the beach is also a small wooden pier, where shuttle boats moor to bring tourists to Skiathos town.

Also Tzaneria has such a beautiful beach, it is located on the other side of the cape of Kanapitsa. Green trees reach also to the beach here and water sports, sun loungers and parasols are available. The only difference lies in the fact that the Tzaneria beach is wider than the beach of Kanapitsa. In Kanapitsa and Tzaneria are several hotels, rooms and apartments for rent. From the main road an hourly bus goes to Skiathos town and to other beaches on the island. In Kanapitsa and Tzaneria live about a hundred permanent residents.

Kanapitsa Holidays Excursions

Sunset Cruise: Admire the stunning scenery and sail across the clear waters of the Aegean Sea and stroll through the local village. Dine at a traditional Greek taverna & stargaze whilst sailing back to port.

Secret Skiathos: The only way to sail around the island in a day and uncover the true mix of beaches and stunning scenery. Why not swim at the famous Lalaria beach, which is one of a few swim stop during the day. Step back in time on visit the old capital Kastro. Remember its a secret.

Aegean Blue: Visit the two neighbouring islands of Skopelos & Alonissos in one day. Go back in time with a guided walk though the narrow streets of Skopelos or relax in a local café and watch the world go by. See the island where Mama Mia was filmed and be your very own Dancing Queen.

VIP Catamaran Experience: For an all inclusive day out relax, soak up the sun and be a VIP for the day. Sailing towards the crystal clear waters of Panormos Bay.

Snorkelling Safari: Discover the underwater world and try to find nemo, in the clear waters surrounding Skiathos. This day will provide you with unforgettable encounters with the underwater world.

Things To See

Fish market and Old port of Skiathos Town: The 'Bourtzi' is situated here. It is a tiny peninsula in the harbour which used to be a Venetians citadel with remains of the 13th century wall and canons.

Monastery of Evangelistria: has some amazing surroundings and is open for the public to visit. Evangelistra also has a small museum with various objects from its history. There is a bus that links the monastery and Chora several times a day.

The medieval capital Kastro: reached by one of the boat trips around the island, or by driving almost all the way and then walking. Don't miss the Church of Christ and the old houses.

Alexandros Papadiamantis Museum: It is the house in which Alexandros Papadiamantis, one of the most important Greek authors of the past century, used to live. The 1st floor is preserved as the house of Alexandros Papadiamantis with its original furniture and objects of the time, whereas the ground floor is functioning as an exhibition room.

Walkabout: Join your reps to meander the small cobble streets of Skiathos town, with a guided tour on some of the hidden treasures and stories and myths behind the town. The first drink is on your rep.

Make your holidays extra special by booking some of our great excursions, places are limited so reserve your place at your Welcome Meeting or contact your holiday representative to avoid disappointment.

Koukounaries

Koukounaries is a small village close to the beach of the same name, it's one of the furthers resorts from Skiathos Town but it's still only 12km away which would take just 20 minutes in the car.

Koukounaries beach is widely considered the best on the island and it can get very busy because of this. The beach offers loungers, beach side tavernas and cafes as well as water sports, pedalo hire and plenty of golden soft sand.

The village of Koukounaries is much smaller than you'd expect being connected to such a popular beach, it's basically a single main road with the amenities dotted along the road. It does of course have a number of restaurants, supermarkets and all the other tourist facilities that you'd expect but it doesn't have a huge amount of night life. Those who want a bit more evening entertainment can always get the bus that runs regularly to Skiathos Town which is 13km away and offers a more lively evenings entertainment. There are 4 bus stops for Koukounaries, 23-26

Those who choose to stay in Koukounaries will be the type that simply want a basic beach break with an evening meal and a carafe of wine rather than those who want to party the night away..

Koukounaries beach

Koukounaries Beach: This is the most famous beach in Skiathos, therefore the most crowded. It is well-known for its extremely fine white sand and its fragrant pine trees forest from which the region took its name. It is considered as one of the best beaches of Greece but was also voted the most unspoiled natural beach of the Mediterranean. The beautiful crystal-clear deep blue waters are a real pleasure. Since the beach is well-organized, it offers many water sports, chairs, umbrellas, beach bars.

The region around the beach is full of restaurants, taverns and some hotel units. A local bus links this beach to the capital every 30 minutes. A biotope can be found in the pine forest boarding the beach where different species of plants and birds are protected. This place, as well as the beach, is developed for ecotourism, financed by the Municipality and the European Union.

Megali Amos

Megali Ammos Beach is located about 1 km outside Skiathos Town. Steep hills that border the area protect the fine sand and light shingle beach from the strong northerly winds offering a calm beach resort. Here you will find plenty of beach activities such as water-skiing. Tavernas restaurants and a well-stocked mini market are located in the area. The town is a labyrinth of small roads and alleys where a walk away from the beach area provides a beautifully authentic feel for local Skiathos life. A lovely location for those seeking a relaxing holiday.

Would you like to be as close to Skiathos Town as possible, but also enjoy the atmosphere of a tourist resort? Why not stay at one of the hotels and studios in Megali Ammos? The area is almost exclusively a summer resort with plenty of traditional or more modern guest houses and hotels. It is the nearest place to Skiathos Town and is easily accessed by foot as it is right next to the Town.

Megali Ammos in Greek means large sand. The name is indicative of the region with its sandy, soft beach extending for many metres along the shore. Due to its location, it is favoured by both locals and tourists who enjoy sunbathing and summer cocktails at the beach bars found here. Adopt a 'when in Greece' attitude and have your lunch at one of the many 'ouzeri' the places where ouzo and small bites of food, called 'mezedes' are served. After going swimming to the clear waters of Megali ammos, enjoying a Greek style meal is by all means worthwhile! It should be followed by a Greek way nap time at the comfortable hotels and studios found right at the beginning of the beach. There is one for everyone's budget.

The resorts are in such a convenient distance from Skiathos Town that you can go out at night and then go back to your room either by foot, bus or taxi without spending a lot of money. In the morning, you can either lie down on your sun lounger and perhaps have a rest after the hangover of the previous night or sign up for water sports at the water sports school which is said to be the most organised of the island. Bear in mind that Megali Ammos can get really busy and crowded especially in the high season, therefore if you prefer some privacy and tranquility, you might need to go to this beach another time. This doesn't make your stay in Megali Ammos less convenient though, as buses run to other beaches regularly. Alternatively, you could hit two birds with one stone and try to go around the rocks towards the east side where there are no sun lounges and umbrellas and the beach is much quieter there.

Enjoy all the benefits of being so close to Skiathos Town and visit Megali Ammos. You will get the best accommodation and facilities in affordable prices without spending a penny for transportation!

Skiathos Town

The capital, Skiathos Town, is a lovely, picturesque town to explore, with whitewashed houses, red-tiled roofs, and tiny lanes, all interspersed with greenery and colorful flowers. For a look at one of the 19th century houses still in existence, and now a museum illustrating the life of Skiathos' most famous citizen, the poet and writer Alexandros Papadiamantis, you need to get off the main street and begin to explore.

The town is full of shops, restaurants, tavernas, and bars. If you were looking for a quiet, uncrowded island capital, you have chosen the wrong island! While the town is delightful to explore, you will not be alone, especially at night.

There are no local crafts which Skiathians produce, but the town has a few nice shops and antique galleries, in addition to the usual number of tourist/souvenir shops. Nightlife abounds in the capital, so you will primarily find yourself at the beach during the day, and pub-crawling at night.

Every island in Greece has its capital town, usually called "Chora". The minute you arrive at the port of Skiathos Town, you realise the captivating beauty of the island. You feel charmed by the spell of the romantic atmosphere of the harbour with the view of the Bourtzi fortress and the mystical green surroundings. The island has a unique cosmopolitan character intertwined in harmony with the tourist attractions and the wild beauty of the nature.

Skiathos Town is the heart of the island. All major events and activities take place here. You will find a large number of restaurants, bars, clubs, shops and other facilities, such as tourist offices and car rentals to make your stay as comfortable as possible. The Town is also reputed for its lively nightlife with lots of young people arriving on the island from all over Greece and overseas to experience unforgettable holidays after graduating either high school or university.

The Town has 5000 residents, but the number of the population increases significantly during the summer months when people who are originally from Skiathos, but have moved to bigger cities for work, return for the summer. The majority of the population are in Skiathos Town, since the rest of the island is barely inhabited. The Town is located in the east part and its geographical position provides a sheltered, windless bay.

Walking down the streets of the Town is an excellent way to spend a relaxed evening on the island and familiarise yourself with its architecture and the locals' way of living. The houses are small and simple, a combination of different styles influenced both by the typical architecture of the islands and the region of Mount Pelion, which dominates the closest mainland city, Volos. In Skiathos Town you will come across Papadiamantis house which operates as a museum. While walking on the pebbled streets of the town, you'll be able to have a look at the souvenir shops or other retail stores jammed in Papadiamantis street. We suggest that you avoid moving around the narrow alleys of the town by car as it is almost impossible if not prohibited.

Apart from the main tourist attractions, such as the Bourtzi fortress or the castle of the Old Town, and the vivid nightlife, when you visit Skiathos

Town, you could also attend some of the various cultural events which take place in the Town in the summer months. The municipality has been organising a cultural festival in the old school inside Bourtzi fortress, which takes place in July and August and is named after the famous story "A Dream On The Wave" by Alexandros Papadiamantis . It doesn't matter if you don't speak Greek. Art is a "lingua franca" that everybody understands in their own way. At the beginning of September another event, called "Violin Days" is organised in honour of the sinking of submarine "Katsonis" during World War II. The history of the Town is associated with World War II. Back then it was bombed and destroyed by the Germans, but the strong spirit of the people of Skiathos survived and they managed to build it from scratch and thrive! These festivals are ideal for culture lovers who want to get acquainted with the Greek literary, musical and cultural traditions.

Skiathos Town is the centre of life on the island. Almost everything takes place here. Book a flight and come see for yourself!

Skopelos Island

Larger than Skiathos and smaller than Skyros, this incredibly green island belongs to the Sporades group, which lie off the eastern coast of the mainland, just north of Evia. You can reach this island by ferry from two mainland ports, Volos and Ai. Konstantinos, which are connected by bus to Athens. You can also fly to nearby Skiathos, and then take one of the frequent ferries across to Skopelos.

It's a beautiful island of 95 square kilometers, carpeted with vegetation and green trees, primarily pines, with an abundance of olive, nut and fruit trees. The island has two ports, Loutraki or Glossa on the northwest coast, and the capital, Skopelos or Chora, on the north coast, about midway along the length of the coast. Since most ferries do stop at both ports, be sure to stay on the boat if you are looking to go to the capital, as that is usually the second stop (or ask a crewmember to be sure that you are disembarking at the right stop).

From Chora there are paved roads leading to the southern beaches and along the west coast as far north as Glossa. A decent bus network, especially in summer, will get you just about everywhere. From stops along the main roads, there are often lovely walks leading down to the beaches, plus great walks along the coast connecting two or more beaches. Plenty of tavernas will be found at most of the main beach/resort areas, but there are also lots of pretty coves offering solitude, privacy, and an ideal environment.

Skopelos has an excellent tourist infrastructure, though the pace and ambience is less frenetic than nearby Skiathos, for instance. Skopelos has encouraged tourism, but not let it run rampant! There are currently about 4,500 year-round inhabitants on the island, who make their living through farming, fishing, and tourism. The fertile land with which the island is blessed, plus an abundance of water, has led to a high level of production of fruit and nuts. Notably are pears, plums, and almonds.

In general, you cannot but be impressed with what nature has endowed to this superb island. For crafts, the island has an important name in ceramic design and production, as well as for a variety of handcrafts, such as weaving and embroidery

Skopelos History

Skopelos island is not just a dreamy place for summer holidays, it is a part of Greece's rich history and cultural heritage. Besides the unique natural beauty that can enchants anyone, the island has historical traces of ancient civilizations, as well as classical and Byzantine monuments that make it more than just an interesting destination.

Through a multitude recordings from the depths of the centuries, may be outlined the form and the identity of Skopelos island. The study of the past, brings to light marks from the first centuries of ancient Greek history. The excavations made in the area of Stafilos during 1936, highlighted findings from the Mycenaean era (15th century B.C.) and connected with the mythical inhabitant Stafilos, son of Dionysos and Ariadne. According to Greek Mythology, Stafilos' brother was Peparithos from whom the island was named from. The Minoan grave, found in the small peninsula of Stafilos, was attributed to the mythical hero and his sword with the golden handle is on display at the National Archaeological Museum.

The 8th century B.C. was the period when Peparithos (Skopelos) was colony of Chalcis, while the traces of ancient city Selinous, on the hill Palaio Kastro in Glossa settlement, demonstrate that this area was inhabited at the same period. As subsequent residents referred the Olympic champion of 569 B.C. Agnontas and the historian of the 3rd century B.C. Dioklis. The findings of excavations on the gulf of Skopelos Town, reveal the existence of a shrine of 4th century B.C. dedicated to Asclepius (god of medicine). Up until now, the operations have revealed amphorae, figured vessels, parts of statues, clay figurines and coins.

From literary sources documented that the island joined in the Athenian alliance (5th and 4th century B.C.), which has contributed significantly to progress and economic prosperity of Peparithos. The development was such that led to cutting silver and copper coins and the contribution of larger amounts to the common fund of the Alliance in comparison with the other islands of the region.

After the end of the Peloponnesian War, Peparithos was under the occupation of the Lacedaemonians and later was an area of conflicts between the Athenians and the Macedonians. Well noted is the event of the occupation of the ancient city of Panormos by Alexander of Feres in 361 B.C. and until the 2nd century B.C. the whole area of Sporades had been taken under the possession of the Macedonians from the Phillip B'. Despite the administrative turmoil, the robust economy of the island wasn't disturbed and the port of Peparithos had been established as a significant part of the market of the Aegean Sea.

The production of a great quality wine, famed from earlier years, spread the trade from the Black Sea to the Alexandria of Egypt. In addition, Peparithos was recognized as an important naval power and its privileged geographical position offered the opportunity to residents to develop naval fleet.

During Roman times the island has experienced several periods of decline mainly due to the conflicts between Greeks and Romans. Archaeological samples of that era are the Roman Baths in the region Loutraki in Glossa and parts of organized laboratories of amphorae manufacturing for the transportation of wine, in rural areas of Stafilos, Agnontas and Panormos. A striking site is also Sentoukia on top of Karya mountain, as well as the myths around the purpose of their creation. There are 3 carved tombs likely from the post Roman years, which have been looted the last century. Although we do not know about their content, the tradition speaks for hidden treasures from pirates' activities in the area.

The Northern Sporades was indeed an area of strong pirate action during the Byzantines and medieval times. Survival purposes forced the population to get involved with the piracy and as a result they developed maritime and shipbuilding art. In addition, the settlements shaped garrison character and were formed on fortified citadels. Samples of fortifications still exist on the north side of Skopelos Town, in the region Kastro (Castle).

The many raids and conflicts weakened the islands and with the invasion of the Turkish fleet in 1538 Skopelos almost deserted.

Several years passed and it was not before the 18th century when the island started to populated again and develop quickly the old commercial activities. Until the beginning of the Greek Revolution, the exports of Skopelos in wine, olive oil and fruits arrived, like old times, in many ports of the eastern but also the western Mediterranean. However, the participation in all of the national fights, for the independence, in the Balkan wars, in the Asian Minor campaign and in the conflicts of World War II, brought changes in the activities of the inhabitants of the island. But it is well worth mentioning the preservation of the old art of shipbuilding until the mid-20th century. The abundant raw material from the pine-tree forests of the island, helped especially in shipbuilding which have gotten a unique form in the hands of locals shipwrights. From the shipyards of island, large ships were sailing to order receivers of other areas. The end of the operations of the yards came with the decline of shipping sailfish and the appearance of the steam boats

Island's Culture

Although the history of the island begins in ancient times, the roots of the culture and traditions that have been integrated in the social structure of the island, comes mostly from the 16th century and onwards.The social features that imposed during the years of the Turkish occupation and has not ceased to exist in subsequent years, directly influenced the traditions, customs and people's culture. The existence social classes disrupted the relationship of residents and maintained a poor as a whole, low standard of living, society. As a result, at the end of the 19th century, there were migratory tendencies toward America, Romania and Russia.

With the travels of residents and in particular of sailors of the island, Skopelos came into contact with other European cultures. The consulates in Skopelos as early as the 18th century like the Venetian, English and France, shows that at a very early stage elements of western culture had invaded the island. So, the new goods that arrived on the island was welcome and the houses slowly acquired furniture, glassware, decorative dishes and various foreign objects. It is worth pointing out that this early assimilation of European features was an exception for the wider area of Sporades.

The specific art forms that developed in Skopelos are reflected in the architecture of the houses, the furniture, the interior decoration, the crafts, the hagiographies and local traditional songs. Features of the rare tradition of the island are the countless legends (with references to foreign conquerors, Saints, exotic creatures and pirates' treasures), the festivals in the chapels, the stories associated with the pastoral life, the carnivals and the intense religious life of residents.

Each person may come into contact with the rich cultural heritage of the island, visiting the Folklore Museum or the Mansion of Vakratsa in Skopelos Town and the Folklore Museum in Glossa. There, in addition to the characteristics of a genuine Skopelos-type home, collections of images, embroidery, paintings, photographs, ceramics, tools and carved wooden furniture saved. Great impression cause the traditional female dress, one of the most important Greek traditional costume, due to the rich appearance and variety of dresses, jewelries and glamorous accessories. The Maritime

Museum and the Museum of Cultural Heritage are two more places that preserve important materials and which is worth visiting.

The feeling of tradition is easily noticeable to the visitor of the island. Apart from the typical architecture of villages, the cultural image of island complemented by the numerous churches and monasteries in the countryside. Overall the temples of Skopelos exceed 150 and many are found between the white pathways of main town. The monasteries are near to 40 and is scattered throughout the lush natural surroundings, hiding impressive relics from previous centuries.

The visitor can easily find the Church of the Nativity of Christ, the Church of the Virgin Mary and the Church of Panagia Faneromeni inside the Town of Skopelos. Also at the same time the visitor can easily reach the picturesque church of Panagia tou Purgou on the cliff NE of the harbor and climb up farthest edge of settlement to meet several other temples such as Agios Athanasios, arriving at the highest point of the Kastro (Castle).

Among the monasteries that caused the admiration of the visitor is the Monastery of Saint Riginos (patron saint of the island) a few kilometers outside Skopelos Town and the Monastery of Evangelistria, the Monastery Metamorfosis, the Monastery of Agia Barbara and the Monastery of Prodromos, all located on the hills opposite the main port of Skopelos. On the other side of Skopelos island, near to Glossa village there is the Monastery of Agioi Taxiarches and the famous (from the Mamma Mia film) Monastery of Agios Ioannis Castri (Saint John Castri), built on top of a huge rock beaten by the waves.

Events

Skopelos Film Festival

The Skopelos International Film Festival for Youth (SIFFY) was first organized in 2009 with the cooperation of Professor Wangtae Lim from Dong-Ah Institute of Media and the Arts and Jill Somer, Associate Director of the Skopelos Foundation for the Arts. Since then, nine festivals have been organized and were funded by private donors through Kickstarter campaigns.

The festival lasts one week to ten days with three days of educational classes based on the yearly theme and then for the next 7 days students work in teams of six to eight with a professional filmmaker to create a short film. The students do everything from creating the initial idea, writing the scenario, camera, directing, acting and then they partially edit the film with the assistance of the professional filmmakers. The last evening the films are screened to the townspeople to an audience of about nine hundred people. The films are then circulated to festivals throughout the world. Films from various years have been screened in America, Asia and Europe.

Glossa Festival

Skopelitians love the dance and it is a way for them to express their connection with the island's tradition. Another Dance Festival is organized by the Cultural and Adornational Association of Glossa Village in the middle of July. For two days, Glossa hosts dance groups and dances at traditional rhythms. Dancers with traditional costumes promote their special culture and give a distinctive color to the cobblestones of the village. Celebrations are repeated in August (at Loutraki - Glossa's port) but also including concerts with famous singers that offers a nostalgic musical journey. In addition, the "Loizia Festival" is held in

August in Glossa, to the honor of Manos Loizos (1937-1982), one of the most important Greek-Cypriot composers of the 20th century. The festival includes concerts with songs of Loizos, theatrical performances, traditional dances and of course food and wine for free.

Rembetiko festival

Skopelos has a long history in music field and has breed great artists. The musical identity of the island was formed by "rebetiko", with the rhythms of which many generations have grown on the island and keep this magnificent kind of music alive. Every year, in the middle of July, a two-day festival is dedicated to the rebetiko with the participation of numerous famous musicians offering to the audience magical summer nights.

Skopelian Week

The Cultural and Folklore Association of Skopelos aim to promote and highlight the local customs, traditions and products of the island and among other summer celebrations organizes the "Skopelian Week". It is a five-day event (during the middle of August), which includes the traditional way of cooking and taste of local products like plums, cheese pie and frumenty and the demonstration of the unique local costume and the traditional wedding ceremony. The events take place on Skopelos port and in the traditional settlement so that the visitor can admire the architecture of "rare beauty" of Chora and tour the picturesque streets of the island.

Skopelos: Excursions and Touring

Beginning with the fabulous capital and port, Skopelos or Chora, there is much to explore and learn about this paradisiacal island. Because Chora is dealt with separately we go on to visit the rest of the island.

From Chora, you can take the paved road south to Stafylos Bay, which is a lovely combination of sand and pebble, some accommodation and tavernas, though a bit crowded in the high summer months. Walking eastward, you can enjoy the clothing optional beach of Velanio. No taverna, but there is a small cantina during high summer. Following the paved road westward from Stafylos, you will reach the small bay and port of Agnondas, also with a bit of accommodation and tavernas, plus caiques departing for the nearby beach and bay of Limnonari, a nearly half-kilometer stretch of fine sand. You can also reach this by footpath in about 20 minutes, and then either return to Agnondas on foot or with caique. Working your way up the west coast on the main road, the next area that you reach will be Panormos, which has now grown into a resort area with water sports and all the bells and whistles you'd expect of a well-developed area. Even though quite built up, it occupies a beautiful setting, has a good sandy beach, and looks across to a tiny, very green islet called Dassia. If you prefer less chaos, do continue on to Milia, possibly the longest sand/pebble beach on the island and one of the best that you'll find anywhere in the Aegean. Here, the pine trees march steeply down the hillside nearly reaching the shore, and you can again see the islet of Dassia in the sea. Continuing up the coast, the next important beach that you see, before reaching the village of Glossa/port of Loutraki, is called Elios. It's a nice long sandy/pebbly beach with a small settlement overlooking it, but it is dramatically backed by beautiful pine-filled hills. If you are using the public bus and combining that with walking, then from here you can catch the trail that leads up to Glossa, passing through the oldest village on the island, Atheato.

The village of Glossa, known for its almond production, sits two kilometers above the port of Loutraki. It's a lovely village of traditional architecture dating to the 18th and 19th centuries, where the island's old customs are still alive, such as the wearing of traditional island garb. The sea views from the village are outstanding, as you might imagine, as is the positioning of the village within the forest. Here there are a few tavernas and Greek coffee shops (kafenia), with a bit of accommodation on offer. Nearby are three towers dating to the 4th century BC. Below, the port of Loutraki also has a small pebbly beach and busy waterfront facilities during high season.

Skopelos Town

Huddled around its perfect horseshoe harbour and clinging to the low hills that rise up from the water, Skopelos Town is all pure white facades, terracotta-red tiled roofs, cerulean blue shutters, jungle green foliage and gun-metal grey flagstones.

It's a charming, uplifting sight for those arriving by boat, a fabulous promise of pleasures to come. Wandering the town's streets and seeing it up close is an equally enjoyable experience. Its labyrinthine web of narrow, traffic-free streets hides innumerable photogenic treasures and picturesque scenes. Tempting tavernas spill out on to shady, vine-covered terraces overlooking the sea, cats bask lazily on sun-warmed steps, tiny churches sound their diminutive bells, reminding neighbours of their religious duties, vigorous bougainvillea flourishes, splashing colour onto white-canvas walls. As the afternoon mellows into evening, bars fill up with thirsty, bronzed beachreturners and then, as darkness falls, restaurants around the harbour buzz with the gentle excitement of convivial pleasures, diners' faces flushed with the soft glow of lanterns and candles.

If your wandering requires focal points, head up to the remains of the 13th century Venetian castle at the top of town. From here the views over the port and out to sea are stunning. Then, as you wind down back towards the harbour, stop off at the Museum of Folklore to find out more about your surroundings. An even better insight into the life of the locals might be had at the lovely portside church of Eisodia tis Theotokou.

During your exploration of Skopelos Town you will come across some great little shops, selling beauty products made from olive oil and honey, artisanal jewellery and crafts, and gastronomic delicacies. Spare a thought for those poor souls who are not with you, and buy them a little bit of Skopelos magic!

The stylistic uniformity of the town's architecture and the integrity of its old town plan was recognised as far back as 1978, when the then President of Greece designated it a Traditional Settlement of Outstanding Beauty. This heritage site status imposes strict building regulations and guarantees that Skopelos Town's intrinsic beauty might be enjoyed by future generations.

Skopelos Tourist Guide

Skopelos has always been my favourite Sporade since a first visit three decades ago. It's the best all-rounder of this group that also includes Skiáthos, Alónissos and Skýros forests and orchards not (yet) too burnt (unlike neighbouring Skiáthos), eminently scenic beaches (pebbly, sandy or both), some excellent tavernas in the harbour hóra (one of the most characterful island towns), plus a not overly packaged feel owing to the lack of an airport. Apparently the honchos in charge of filming Mamma Mia! thought so too, choosing Skopelos as the main shooting location during September 2007. Inevitably locals have cashed in on this with Mamma Mia! boat tours and such, but it's hardly overpowering.

As on all the Sporades, there is scant evidence of ancient times, so the beach-flopping sybarite can flop without missing enormous cultural edification aside from the main town, a few scattered villages and rural monasteries. Geologically, geographically and mentality-wise Skopelos and its neighbours are extensions of mainland Magnesia province and specifically Mt Pílion; musical tastes are firmly urban rather than Aegean, and medieval settlement from the Ionian islands (after Ottoman admiral Barbarossa slaughtered all the previous inhabitants in 1539) fostered a style of Italianate singing.

A distinctive feature of the countryside are prune-drying ovens, scattering next to orchard cottages with their beaked chimneys. Skopelos was once noted for its prune-plums, but the late-summer, labour-intensive, kneaded-by-hand drying process was uneconomical compared to the chemically assisted California product, so the industry largely died out by the 1980s.

For such a lush island, Skopelos has water problems (specifically an undrinkable, extraordinarily hard mains supply), aggravated by new villa complexes near Hóra. If you like to fill up canteens rather than waste money (and litter the landscape) with plastic mineral-water bottles, potable springs are at Metóhi near Evangelistrías convent, above Stáfylos beach and in the Karyá ravine en route to the Sendoúkia tombs.

Hóra And Around

Hóra drapes itself over the westerly slope closing off a broad, north-facing bay, with a ruined Venetian castle up top; tiers of imposing, often slate-roofed mansions and churches reputedly 123 of the latter, including frequent postcard star Panagítsa tou Pýrgou reveal themselves to arriving boats rounding the headland. Away from the inevitable waterside commercial strip, the town is decidedly time-warped, with wonderfully idiosyncratic shops of a sort long vanished elsewhere in Greece. Domestic architecture, including some superb arcades and balconied facades, is largely unadulterated with tasteless monstrosities as on most other islands. For more on the local building style, see French Skopelophile Marc Held's illustrated Skopelos: The Landscapes and Vernacular Architecture of an Aegean Island (sold locally).

The municipal car-park and KTEL area on the jetty was once the site of thriving, picturesque boatyards. The great Thessalian photographer Takis Tloupas and my humble self captured them in action as late as 1981, but like the prune industry they have since vanished; unlike Skiáthos, Skopelos no longer makes traditional boats on any scale.

Hóra has the best tavernas on the island, and it's easy to avoid the tourist-traps with their photo-menus at mid-quay. As a general (if not infallible) rule, the best dining experiences are to be had on the far, northwest quay. Cheap but drinkable bulk or bottled wine hails from the Dimitra cooperative at Néa Anhíalos, while Apostolakis products mark a step up in quality. Englezos does the standards with an original twist; the menu changes seasonally but www.englezos.gr gives an idea of current offerings. The very last building on the quay is Kymata (aka Angelos), probably the oldest taverna in town and a shrine of magireftá dishes like lamb and vegetables in a phyllo crust and beets with their greens; one lunchtime here in 2007 I was treated to the spectacle of two old fishermen conversing in mantinádes (rhyming couplets), a practice which has largely died out away from Crete. The top seafood venue is Klimataria, next to the dimarhío(city hall), with affordable per-kilo prices for local, non-farmed fish. Inland, Gorgones is the only genuine ouzerí in town, with indoor/outdoor seating, fair prices and year-round operation.

Among after-hours options, one that stands out and up is unsigned Anatoli, at the very summit of the kástro, where veteran rebétika musician Yiorgos Xintaris performs (and sells a worthwhile CD) from late June to early September only, when his sons (who accompany him) return from university. Large parties should reserve on tel: 24240 22851.

On Mt Paloúki, flanking the bay on the east, stand three historic monasteries. Evangelistrías (daily 8am–1pm & 5–8pm), visible from town and founded in 1712 as an ecclesiastical academy by the Daponte family, is notable more for the katholikón's architectural details than its two rather gormless nuns, bundled in here as young girls 60 years ago. Secluded Prodhrómou (same hours), occupied by a trio of more with-it sisters, was largely destroyed in the March 1965 earthquake which lashed the Sporades, but preserves fine icons. Sixteenth-century Metamórfosis, an Athonite dependency at the top of a verdant ravine, is being seasonally restored when its surly caretaker monk is about, a process hopefully leaving untouched a colourful dome upheld by four dark coral-rock columns.

In the opposite direction from Hóra, the Palio Karnagio taverna at small sand-and-pebble Glystéri cove a Mamma Mia! location is popular at weekends. A turning from the Glystéri road leads west via the lush Karyá valley, along the east flank of 681-metre Mount Dhélfi to the well-marked Sendoúkia, three cyst-type Hellenistic graves with their lids knocked askew by tomb-raiders. They're a short hike away first on path, then a cairned cross-country route; the views over Alónissos and minor islets, especially at dusk, make the trip worthwhile.

Alphonse The Philhellene Spy

Foreign dropouts, well before the hippies of the 1960s, have a long history in Greece. Among the first was Austrian Alphonse, an ostensible fisherman who pottered around Skopelos in a little boat from 1937 to 1939, roistering in the cafés with the island fisherman until one day after a storm, when his wooden boat was found smashed on a remote shore. But the fisher-persona and drowning/disappearance had all been staged; when the Germans took over as occupiers from the Italians in autumn 1943, the officer at the head of the column marching into town was none other than Alphonse. He repaid the islanders' prior hospitality by ensuring that unlike Skiáthos and Alónissos, where Nazi reprisals were severe no harm befell Skopelos, despite the fact that a fair number of the local men had joined the resistance in the Píndos mountains. After the war, Alphonse returned to live out his days (until 1987) drinking with a different set of fishermen at Tríkeri on the tip of the Pílion peninsula.

South & West Coast Beaches Of Skopelos

Stáfylos, 4km from Hóra, is the closest proper beach, though small and crowded, with a single, merely adequate taverna at road's end. Better to walk five minutes east over the headland to more scenic, sand-and-pea-gravel Velanió, 600m long with a nudist zone and a seasonal kantína.

Agnóndas, about 3km west, has a small beach but mostly serves as an alternate ferry port; among several tavernas, best is Pavlos, for seafood, unusual mezédes like tsitsírava (pickled terebinth shoots) and Apostolakis bulk wine. There's better, white sand at Limnonári cove just to the west.

As the coastline bends to face west rather than south, the first substantial place is Pánormos bay, popular with yachts owing to its abundant, protected anchorage, somewhat less so with bathers owing to a steeply shelving, gravelly shore. Just around the corner, Miliá beach(photo)is superior, with two 400-metre arcs of tiny pebbles opposite Dhassía islet separated by a headland with a sometimes noisy beach bar at the south cove. Parking in season is impossible unless you patronize the single, fortunately good taverna with its private lot. Kastáni beach, immediately north with its own access drive, was a major Mamma Mia! location but despite this is far calmer, with a naturist zone and no amenities besides a kantína working out of a converted bus. There are more secluded beaches at Hóvolo, outside otherwise dreary Élios (Néo Klíma) village, built to rehouse victims of the 1965 quake, and Armenópetra, with the ship-shaped rock of the name just offshore.

Far Northwest Skopelos

The island trunk road, have passed all the aforementioned beaches, climbs back to civilisation of sorts at Paleó Klíma, the village worst affected by the earthquake and abandoned thereafter, helped along by the junta declaring it unfit for habitation, closing the school and making it almost impossible to get a power hookup. The place was subsequently bought up and restored in variable taste by Greek and foreign outsiders, but it never really thrived in its new incarnation, and there's currently no bakery, taverna or shop. The main attraction is the start of a wonderful 45-minute path, via Ágii Anárgyri hamlet (also bought up and restored) to Athéato, the oldest settlement on Skopelos, barely glimpsing the sea in an attempt to be pirate-proof but with some fine vernacular architecture attracting more sensitive restoration. I almost purchased a house here in 1992; it's still there, unsold, so the legal problems must have proven as I then suspected insurmountable.

Athéato lies just east of Glóssa, Skopelos' second largest village, 26km from Hóra, with sweeping views across the straits to Évvia. It's a countrified, ramshackle place stacked in terraces, with lush gardens between the houses. To Agnandi is the (overpriced) koultouriárika taverna, but most locals gravitate instead towards whole roast goat or lamb on a spit at To Steki tou Mastora at the town entrance by the church. A twisty road, and a much briefer cobbled path, lead down to the dozy port of Loutráki, which takes its name from some very ruined Roman baths nearby. There's accommodation here if you need to catch an early ferry, but the tiny beach and three tavernas prove equally unmemorable.

Better beaches are found nearby on the north coast at Perivolioú, with rock overhangs for shade, and at Hondroyiórgis, both reached by dirt tracks. A separate, paved road leads to the local photo-op of Ágios Ioánnis Kastrí (photo), a church perched atop a rock pinnacle conquered by steps; an equally steep path nearby leads down to a decent sandy cove.

Recommended Walking Maps And Guides

Two commercial topographic maps cover Skopelos, both at 1:25,000 scale: one issued by Anavasi (www.anavasi.gr), the other by Terrain (www.terrainmaps.gr). The latter is much newer and likely to be better, as the Anavasi researcher didn't cooperate with local guide Heather Parsons (tel 694 5249328, www.skopelos-walks.com), author of Skopelos Trails and leader of guided hikes in spring/autumn. She gets, unfortunately, very little support from locals, and the number of quality walking opportunities is steadily being reduced by thoughtless bulldozing of old cobbled trails and illegal fencing. An unflattering comparison with Alónissos, where EU money has been skilfully deployed by locals and foreigners working together to rehabilitate an extensive trail network.

Skopelos Accommodation

While few Athens travel agencies work directly with the island of Skopelos, Dolphin Hellas Travel, Fantasy Travel and Aegean Thesaurus Travel does have a number of properties they cooperate with and with the difficult route you have to take to get to the island it is not a bad idea to work with a travel agent. If you plan to combine Skopelos with other islands or destinations on the mainland I suggest you use Matt's Create-an-itinerary form which allows you to choose the islands, the number of days and get a price with no obligation to purchase.

Among the hotels recommended…

Blue Green Bay
Showcasing an outdoor pool and views of the sea, Blue Green Bay is located in Panormos Skopelos, a one minute walk from the beach. Each one of the 16 Blue Green Bay's rooms, apartments, studio and maisonette are viewing the tranquil crystal clear turquoise waters of a small bay, with the stunning natural beauty and vegetation. They offer facilities like air conditioning (individually controlled), flat TV set and direct dial phone, Wi-Fi internet access, mini fridge, hair dryer, bath amenities and welcome local delicacies. From your private veranda or balcony, you have the privilege of enjoying the view of a stunning beauty offered

by the little natural harbor called "Blo", as well as a magical sunset.

Hotel Rigas

Located in Skopelos Town, Hotel Rigas features a garden and seasonal outdoor pool. All units are air conditioned and feature a TV. Some units include a terrace and/or balcony with pool views. There is also a kitchenette in some of the units fitted with a refrigerator. Crossing the entrance of the main yard with the giant bougainvillea, you are flooded from the scent of lemon, mandarin trees and night flowers that provide a cool shade to the ground-floor rooms of the main building. Its aesthetics and design bring to mind the image of the sunny courtyards of Spanish villas.

Skopelos Holidays Hotel & Spa

Featuring free WiFi, a seasonal outdoor pool and asun terrace, Skopelos Holidays Hotel & Spa offers accommodations in Skopelos Town. Guests can enjoy the on-site restaurant and every room at this hotel is air conditioned and has a TV with satellite channels. This hotel offers all modern amenities, a fitness center, and the rejuvenation pleasures you always wished to offer yourself, but the pace of the city life deprived you from. The unique atmosphere by the pool and the private gardens, ensures relaxing moments with refreshing drinks at the pool bar, and tasteful experiences at the hotel's restaurant. And with more than 2 generations of experience on weddings planning, a group of professionals will help you create an event perfectly in tune with your own taste, style and budget.

Elios Holidays Hotel
Families love the Elios Holidays Hotel in Neo Klima. Guests can enjoy the on-site restaurant and pool and rooms with sea and mountain views. Built in local architecture on a scenic terrain, embraced by

thick pine forests, the hotel is just 500 meters away from the sandy - pebbly magnificent beaches of Elios and Hovolo, and near to Kastani and Milia beaches, acclaimed after the "Mamma Mia" film.Flowers, plants and a huge pine scatter particular color and shade on site while the furnished pool deck assembles the most unwinding and carefree moments. All our little guests shall pumper at the children's pool and lush open grounds. Neo Klima is an uncrowded and convenient tourist resort, an excellent base for all visitors who want to explore the island, and the numerous beautiful west coast beaches.

Panorama Studios is located on the hillside overlooking Skopelos Town in the area of Aghios Konstantinos. This quaint family-owned and operated property is made up of traditional rooms which can accommodate couples and families. All of the rooms are spacious and offer fantastic sea views from their furnished balconies. Each room comes with a mini-fridge and kitchenette with cooking and eating utensils.

Skopelos Village is a luxury hotel where Mamma Mia! crew stayed with an outdoor pool and playground. Adrina Resort & Spa is located in Panormos just a 5 minute walk from the beach. The B-Catagory Hotel AMALIA is on the sea, only 500 meters from the port of Skopelos. The B-Catagory Aperitton Hotel is a model of contemporary and traditional local architecture, 200 meters from the port and the town beach. Showcasing an outdoor pool and sun terrace, Anofli Suites is located in Skopelos Town a few steps away from the beach. Just a few metres away from the sea in Neo Klima 1 minute walk from the beach in Neo Klima, Studios and Apartments Meri features a garden, barbecue, and sun terrace.

Aegean Wave Hotel in Loutraki offers panoramic sea views from its lovely sun terrace. This charming hotel is just 200 metres from the sea and features free Wi-Fi. Situated on the hillside of Loutraki and overlooking the sea and the port, Hotel Selenunda offers spacious self-catering apartments with sea views, making it an ideal base for exploring Skopelos. Hovolo Apartments are situated on the coastal road in Neo Klima village in Scopelos, at a distance of about 130 metres from the beach. The popular beach of Hovolo is also within easy reach from the complex. The Hotel Denise is built in an ideal spot of the main village of Skopelos as it offers a panoramic view as well as an easy access though the peripheral road or through the picturesque narrow streets.

Getting To And Around Skopelos

There is no flat ground for an airport. Skiáthos has the closest one, but check connecting ferry or catamaran departures carefully or you risk being stranded, especially with evening arrivals.

Skopelos, surprisingly considering its modest size, has three ports: at Hóra, Loutráki and Agnóndas on the south coast, the latter used during northerly storms and potentially by the summer-only line to Thessaloníki. From the mainland, the principal departure ports are Vólos and Ágios Konstandínos. From each, a mix of conventional boats or jet ferries (taking cars) and hydrofoils (foot passengers only) plies 3 times daily in mid-summer, dropping to at most 2 daily in spring/autumn and about 5 weekly offseason. For Ágios departures, Alkyon Travel in central Athens provides a linking coach service a few hours before or you can book a taxi with George the Famous Taxi Driver. You can find ferry schedules at Ferryhopper.com

There are various car- and scooter-hire places in Hóra. KTEL buses from the main ferry quay ply the main longitudinal road to Glóssa and Loutráki several times daily, passing all the southwesterly beaches (or the side-tracks to them) en route. Taxis cluster next to the KTEL terminal. Except to Glystéri, taxi-boat services are absent, and be aware that day-trips advertised to the Sporades Natural Marine Park are a con you'll spend more than half of the advertised 8-hour duration in transit. Visit the marine park from Alónissos much closer and they need the business more anyway

Skyros Island

Welcome to the island of the co-existence of the most contrasting opposites: Green pine forests combined with harsh, arid wilderness, traditional customs together with modern infrastructure, pious, reverent Christians being transformed into

Dionysian festival participants, the most appealing myths together with the most appalling historic adventures; unbreakable ties with the past immersed into the dawn of mankind, sustaining a present full of aspirations for the future.

Twenty-four miles away from the coast of Euboia and its port of Kymi lies Skyros. You may have come here by plane or on board the "Achilles" ferry, after a one and a half -hour relaxing voyage. Some 2600 people, trying to make a living on fisheries, animal husbandry and tourism, are here to help you, but, at the same time, they respect your privacy and let you relax and enjoy your vacation.

The very name of the island, Skyros, comes from the ancients, as the island was called by the same name thousands of years ago. There are fantastic beaches if you like to work on your tan and swim, wild coastlines if you prefer rock diving or snorkeling and exploring the marvels of the sea bed. There are innumerable, interesting walking trails, should you like to explore the Mediterranean maquis vegetation of the scrubland in the southern part of the island, which is composed primarily of leathery, broad-leaved evergreen shrubs or thorny bushes. Its imposing castle and its history, the numerous chapels, and the old episcopal church up in the 9th century fortress are thrilling attractions for the visitor and cultural jewels for the island and its people.

Whether windsurfing, spear fishing or tracer fishing, beach sports, scuba diving, sailing, trekking, museum visits, sea cave exploration, clubbing until dawn, or just reading a book, all will contribute to an unforgettable visit.

History of Skyros

The history of Skyros, millenia long and adventurous, is not very different to the one of the Aegean Sea as a whole. Good times and bad times, prosperity and impoverishment, freedom and slavery, heroism and cowardness, not unlike anywhere else in Greece, it is interesting to the travelers wanting to acquire some background knowledge about the place they choose to spend their vacations at.

Prehistoric Era

In Gournes Acropolis and in Ahilli cove remnants of the late Palaeolithic era have been found. Neolithic settlements were found in Tou Papa To Houma and a bit more to the North, in Magazia, while in Pouria there has been an Early Bronze Age settlement. The Early Bronze Age had been a time when the island's economy prospered; its Northern part was densely populated. Settlements were scattered from the eastern slopes of the acropolis as far as Ta Gyrismata, an area roughly identical with the inhabited area of today. Early Bronze Age relics were also found in Atsitsa, Koumari and St. Phokas. In Kartsinoudi, Markessi, Hartza and the Alykos Coves obsidian articrafts found might be proof that there, too, existed such settlements.

A very important discovery was made in the northern side of Palamari Cove, at a place known as Kastraki (Small Castle). Megaron-style houses, with perfectly preserved internal architectural structures dated to the late 3rd and early 2nd millenia B.C., were unearthed. A rich collection of almost intact household items found in deeper layers permit a thorough study of the population's way of life and technical equipment available.

Middle Bronze Age is very difficult to document in Skyros. Some Meso-Helladic "ostraca", together with Early Bronze Age ones, were found in Tou Papa To Houma, Molos, Polichri, Atsitsa, while in Palamari building traces were identified.

There is no archaeological evidence for the Mycenaean Kingdom of Skyros, although this is well known from the literary tradition and the myths related to it, as well as from the Mycenaean pottery collected from the cemeteries around the acropolis. It is certain that the small settlement on the acropolis hill, as early as the Copper Age, acted as the nucleus for the Mycenaean settlement, and little by little it became the center for all eventual habitation of the island.

Mythical evidence

The first people to inhabit Skyros have been the Thracian Pelasgi, who made their appearance here around 2500-1900 B.C. They, also here, built the Pelasgic (Cyclopean) walls. Pelasgi are known to be present here when the island was occupied by the Athenians in 475 B.C., after their victory over the local Dolopes. But, long before this, Pelasgia, as the island was named after the Pelasgi, was occupied by the Cares, who originated from Asia Minor Caria. Many of the Pelasgi were obliged to flee to Attica and Megaris as refugees. Among them were the ancestors of Theseus, who eventually managed to climb up the social ladder and become part of the Athenian ruling class.

Cares were chased away by the Sovereings of the Aegean, the Cretans, under the leadership of Rodamanthes, who conquered the islands of the Archipelago; the islands were distributed to the Cretan allies and fellow warriors. Peparethos (Skopelos) was offered to Staphylos, and Skyros to Anyeas, son to Dionysus and Ariadne. It was during his rule that all settlements on Skyros were united in one state under his sovereignty. He had the city/castle fortified by strong walls.

During the era of the Minoan Civilization, Skyros made big steps in progress. It was the time that Cretan colonists built Krission in Kalamitsa region. The island's population increased to a level difficult to believe, local enmities ceased, vineyards and olive tree cultivation was well established; Cretans brought along and propagated their advanced Minoan civilization, their religion and their economic system.

After the destruction of the Minoan civilization and the Cretan sea sovereignty declined, around 1540 B.C., Cretans were chased away or subordinated to the new Sovereigns of Greece, Achaeoi, who came to the island crossing the strait from Euboia or the neighboring islands. A group of Achaeoi, named Dolopes, landed Skyros, put it under their rule, and were in control for many centuries. The island was renamed to Dolopia, as we have previously mentioned.

This is the era of Mythological heroes, like Enyeus, Lykomedes, Achilles, Neoptolemos, and Theseus. Skyros was visited by many a renowned kings, respected for their prudence, bravery or even their slyness, like Odysseus, Nestor, Lykomedes, Phoenix, and Diomedes. During the Trojan War, the king of Skyros was Lycomedes, a Dolope descendant, brother of Thetis, Peleus' wife and Achilles' mother. It was here that Achilles spent his youth, had an affair with Deidameia, daughter of Lycomedes' and had a son by her named Neoptolemos. Prophecy said that the son of Thetis would have either a long but dull life, or a glorious but brief one. When the Trojan War broke out, Thetis was anxious and concealed Achilles, disguised as a girl, at the court of Lycomedes, but her trick was revealed by Odysseus, and Achilles, king of Myrmidons, did take part in the war that would mean his death. Achilles sailed to Troja from a small port of the island which was named after him, Achilli (or Ahilli), and it has the same name until today.

Other myths (and more credible ones, one must admit) have it that Dolopes were subordinate to the king of Thessaly, Peleus, but Lycomedes rebelled and tried to gain his autonomy. Achilles, son of Peleus' and his successor, campaigned against him in command of his Myrmidons, defeated him, got control of his castle and killed him. Many prisoners were taken, among whom was Lycomedes' virgin daughter, Iphis, whom Achilles donated as a gift to his friend Patroclus. Homer, in his masterpiece The Iliad, refers to Iphis as the mistress of Patroclus'.

Historical Times

Skyros was colonized by Chalkideans and Athenians. Chalkideans came first, during the 8th and 7th centuries B.C., on their way to their expansion to Macedonia and Thrace. They needed to have their backs safe, so they got control of Skyros and Euboic Kymi.

As a result of the Lelandian war, Dolopes took Skyros again, until they were thrown out by the Athenians. The island was divided into parcels that were given out to Athenians by lottery, making sure in this way that there would always be a vigilant eye for the Athenian interests. It was then that Kimon searched and found the grave of Theseus and brought his bones back to Athens in great honors.

The island imported customs from Athens: Athenian names were given to towns and ports, and Athenian traditional public holidays and manifestations were held here as well. A new city was built on the castle's north side, and the old city was turned into a fortified acropolis. A new small port was built as well, where Skala Agiou Dimitriou exists today.

During the Peloponnesian War, Athenians lost hold of Skyros and the island became autonomous in 404 BC. Later on, the Athenians came back to power, until the city was taken by Syllas, and Skyros became a Roman possession. During the Roman times Skyros remained in the dark. During the pestilence of 165 AD. the island's population was decimated. In 268 AD. Erouloi and Goths plundered Skyros and Lemnos, as well as the eastern coastline of the mainland.

Byzantine Times

During this period Skyros belonged to the Byzantine Empire, and its inhabitants turned Christian. The first Christian community was established at the end of the 2nd century. The first Christians were responsible for the complete destruction of ancient works of Art, temples, altars and statues. This vandalism was much worse than any damage done to the island by all the past plunderers of Skyros taken together! Numerous Christian churches were built at the expense of construction materials taken from ancient Greek public buildings.

During this period Skyros was used by the Byzantine authorities as a place of exile for various public servants who fell into disfavor with high-ranking officials. These people usually spent all their life on Skyros, creating families and bringing wealth and culture to the island. Skyros was safe and in peace for long periods of time encouraging the growth of folk arts: pottery, wood carving, weaving, embroidery, all of which flourished. In 825 Arabs from Andalusia conquered Crete, establishing a big pirate kingdom which plundered the islands and the mainland coasts, and Skyros, together with the rest of the Aegean, underwent material and human damages. Cities were destroyed and their populations decimated, all but the fortified acropolises, difficult to be taken by assault. The Saracens established a lair in Saraceno and inflicted heavy losses and widespread damage to Skyros and the rest of the Aegean islands. This lasted until 961, when Byzantine Emperor Nikiphoros Phokas reconquered Crete, and the pirates were thus deprived of their stronghold.

Medieval Times

After Constantinople's fall to the Frank Crusaders, the Aegean islands were given to the Venetians;

conquering them would be impossible to a city of merchants, so Venetian authorities urged individuals to establish Venetian colonies wherever serious profits could be expected. Marco Sanudo set off with a handful of ships with a bunch of fortune-hunting mercenaries on board and managed to conquer 17 islands and establish the Frankish Dukedom of the Aegean, with Naxos as its capital. The Aegean islands were offered as lute to Sanudo's knight fellow fighters and were grouped in timars, under twenty new dynasties. Skyros, together with Skopelos, Alonnissos, Skiathos, Kea, Tinos and Mykonos were given away to the Gizi brothers, Venetian merchants. Long-lasting family quarrels resulted in Skyros becoming a lair of piracy of one of the Gizi brothers' descendants against his kin.

In 1269 Skyros revolted against the Franks and, until 1296, it remained under the rule of Michael

Palaeologos, emperor of Byzantium. The island was then taken back by the Franks. Twelve years later, in 1308, the Catalan war fleet, consisting of 60 galleys led by Ferdinand of Majorca, sailed against the islands of the region. After they had attacked, plundered and destroyed Skopelos, they headed towards Skyros, but were met by a seastorm and all of the ships, but one, sunk with all hands on board, and the island was saved.

The complete destruction of the pirate fleet was due, according to the local people, to a miracle by St. Georgios, savior of the island. It was only the galley of Chief pirate Ferdinand that was saved, but it went ashore to Skyros and, according to the tradition, it was petrified and turned into a huge rock one can still see near Achilli (Ahilli), north of Kochyla.

Later on Dallecarceri, Duke of Naxos, had the island's castle fortified, to fight back attacks by the Genoese and Turks. It was then that the dark dungeon in the castle was turned into the first cistern of the island, to provide the guard with water. More cisterns were built at Tris Boukes port and Kalamitsa, all meant to provide water to the local guard forces.

Between 1400 and 1450 pirate attacks destroyed Skyros. Castles were destroyed to the ground, defending walls were demolished, houses burnt down, many of the island's inhabitants taken away and sold as slaves. The population was heavily decimated and rural regions were deserted. The ones that were spared gathered to two destitute villages, Kastro and Markezina, possibly also Palaeokastro, to lead their miserable lives.

After the fall of Constantinople in 1453, Skyros was reconquered by the Venetians and, in the 1454 Treaty, their rule was recognized by the Sultan. After the fall of Constantinople the people in the Sporades islands were helpless against the pirates and the Turks, and preferred the Venetian rule, offering themselves and their islands to the Venetian admiral Loredan, on condition they would be allowed to keep their former privileges and the episcopal seat.

In 1470 a great assault of the Turkish admiral Mahmut Pasha against Skyros, on his way to Chalkis, failed.

The Venetians remained in Skyros until 1537. During their rule, there existed some just governors and others, who did not respect the rights of the people of Skyros, and their decisions were blatantly arbitrary.

Turkish Rule

During the late 15th and early 16th centuries the Aegean in particular, but the Atlantic as well, were in the stronghold of the feared pirates, the Barbarossa brothers. One of them, the infamous red-bearded Barbarossa Hayreddin Pasha was so successful that he eventually became a Turkish Admiral and fought many battles in favor of the Ottoman Sultan all over the Mediterranean. He and his ships attacked, massacred, plundered, chained and sold as slaves in the Muslim slave markets the Christian inhabitants of practically all the Aegean islands and coastal towns and villages, not to mention the Mediterranean ones, then under the Venetians. The Sporades Islands were no exception. Although Skyros was ceded to him by treaty, his crew continued with slaughter, plunder and arson. It was the year of 1539. Many of the inhabitants were forced to flee the island

and find refuge on Euboia, in Kymi. Most of them returned home when the danger was over.

When the island was finally under the Turks, raids stopped and life could go on without any major catastrophies. The population was purely Greek, and despite the heavy taxation, Skyros could keep its autonomy and self-government.

In 1647, the Venetian fleet of 90 ships under admiral Grimani used Skyros as a lair, waiting for the Turkish fleet to come by. Three years later the Venetian fleet under Leonardo Foscolo attacked the island, conquered the castle, demolished it and killed all the Turkish garrison. They took 11 canons and a lot of Skyrians, who were obliged to serve as oarsmen in their galleys. On the island only old men, women and children were left.

The people had to rebuild the castle, which had served as their safety. It is there that food was kept for the sometimes prolonged sieges and Skyrian families kept their precious belongings. Agriculture should start over, and so did animal husbandry (mainly sheep and goats). Nevertheless, Venetian threat was not over. In 1667, the Venetian admiral Morosini, sailing out from Crete, inflicted a lot of damage to Cyclades and Skyros. It is the same man who bombarded the Athens Parthenon and resulted in its partial destruction and plundering of the artifacts, demolished by the explosion.

In 1770 many Skyrians were taken by force to man the crews of the fleet under the Orlof, the Russian admiral who attacked and inflicted heavy damage to the Turkish armada at Tsesme.

As from 1809, the people of Skyros were obliged to offer a certain number of individuals to serve as sailors in the Turkish navy every year. Very little is known of the existence of a Turkish colony on Skyros: Some foreign traveler's have left written testimony of it; that some Turkish families were established in some villages, that a mosque was built on Skyros, and that there also existed a Turkish cemetery where the Gymnastics grounds of the First Elementary School are today. At the cemetery a tomb stone was unearthed, with an inscription in Arab-Turkish, kept today at the Skyros Archaeological Museum. Whoever these were, they must have left the island when pirate attacks intensified. Only Ottoman officials were left, the local Governor having also police duties. They had some men in their command, Turkish gendarmes (zaptiehs) and the Judge (The qadi).

After the Turkish-Russian war, these officials also left, with the exception of the qadi. Only short-time visits of Turkish tax collectors with their sentinels were paid. When the Greek Merchant

Navy, having hoisted the Russian flag, began to develop, and pay frequent visits to Skyros, also the qadi was withdrawn. Judicial duties were undertaken by three elected elderly men called "Demogerontes", an institution that flourished during Turkish rule and was abolished by Kapodistrias in 1830. Their superior judicial authority was the Bishop of Syros. Turkish soldiers had no right to set foot on Skyros with the exception of the yearly visit of the Tax-collectors from Constantinople.

A few years before the Greek Revolution against the Turkish rule broke out, this situation gradually changed. Armed rebels coming from Mainland Greece, as far as Macedonia, as well as refugees from nearby Euboia, gathered on Skyros seeking safety. In 1816, five years prior to the uprising, on Skyros there were 760 armed Greeks and Muslim Albanians to which the island offered its hospitality. Those Albanians, known as Liapides, used to serve the Turkish army as mercenaries but, for various reasons, turned anti-Turkish and were welcome to assist the Greek warriors. Because of some not worth mentioning quarrel, the Liapides turned against the defenseless locals, inflicting indescribable harm: looting, arson of most of the island's households, rape and abduction of young girls and women to turn them into slaves. Many Skyrians, not able to cope with such rapacity and atrocity, fled to Psara, Smyrne (Izmir), or elsewhere, only to come back during or after the war of Independence of 1821-1828.

Skyros, although a small island, contributed to the war substantially, in terms of both money and human life. Skyros always offered refuge to Greek armed warriors, to recover from their wounds and regroup for the continuation of the struggle. Three hundred Albanian mercenaries were hired for the island's protection but another three hundred Greek warriors under various Greek commanders received the island's hospitality.

Modern Times

Skyros gained Freedom together with the rest of The Sporades Islands in 1829 and joined the rest of Greece in good and bad times. Today Skyros has managed to maintain the local cube-like residential architecture, providing in this way an open air museum of building tradition. Folk art and its tradition, wood-carving, ceramics, weaving and needlework, all based on decorative motifs from the local natural and social surrounding, are still alive and continue today. Many other folk traditions are also kept alive, peaked by the Skyrian Carnival Festivities, which remind one of Dionysian worship and the ages-old wish of Man to strengthen the revitalizing forces of Nature.

Skyros Cities and Towns

Gyrismata

The area of Gyrismata in Skyros is one that is very popular during the summer season. Visitors from all over the island head to here to enjoy the beautiful sandy beach and the blue and green waters of the Aegean sea.

Located on the north east coast, just a short distance from the main town of Chora, Gyrismata is easily accessible, and visitors will be rewarded by the charming scenery and landscapes that surround the area.

Though small in comparison to some of the other resorts and towns spread out around Skyros, Gyrismata has a certain charm and magic about it.

This makes it a very attractive place to visit for those who are seeking somewhere to enjoy very relaxed and peaceful holidays in Skyros.

There is a small selection of traditional tavernas where you can enjoy a freshly prepared meal.

With this part of Skyros being very popular with visitors, you can find a lovely range of hotels in Gyrismata as well as other accommodation such as studios and apartments, many of which are very close to the sea.

Magazia

The wonderful coastal resort of Magazia is a favourite destination for visitors to the island of Skyros. The town is located very close to the town of Chora, and it's dark sand beach make it a very popular area during the summer months.

Magazia is actually considered by many to be the beach part of the town of Chora, which is located on the mountain overlooking the beach. The scenery of Magazia is much as it was years ago, with development taking place here, but on a smaller scale than some other parts of the island. This has helped Magazia preserve much of it's traditional apperance and feel.

The name of the town is said to have come from the gunpowder magazines that were once stored here during the Venetian times.

Visitors to this part of the island will find a great selection of accommodation including apartments and rooms to let. During the summer seaon, Magazia can get quite busy, though not as crowded as some of the other more famous Greek holiday destinations.

Visitos to the area of Perasmata in Magazia should try to pay a visit to the charming church of Agios Georgios. There are some other churches and places of interest in Magazia for visitors.

For those planning on staying here in Magazia, there are a nice selection of afe bars and restaurants where you can enjoy a meal or drink, as well as some other local shops where one can stock up on various necessities.

The neighbouring area of Molos seems almost connected to Magazia, as though they are one and the same towns. Molos begins where Magazia ends, and the two coastal towns compliment each other perfectly.

With a great selection of accommodation including studios, apartments and hotels in Magazia, you can easily find the perfect choice for your holidays.

Skyros Town

Skyros Town: Perched on the side of a mountain overlooking a beautiful harbor, Chora is truly spectacular with white Cycladic style cube houses stacked on top of each other.

The meandering roads lead to ther central square of the village. The whole town is crowned by the

Castle, a Byzantine fortress with some Venetian trimmings built over the ancient acropolis. Following the signs from there, tourists will reach the main square, which lies on the way to the Castle. On the way you will pass the church of Agia Triada which hosts some fine frescoes as well as the white monastery of Agios Georgios founded in 962 AD.

Pano Piatsa or the Upper Square in the center of this serene, quaint town is the city center. The center has many inns and taverns offering beverages and delicacies, as well as bars and cafes. It is here, perched on a terrace overlooking the beach, you will find the bronze Statue of Immortal Poetry erected in 1931 to commemorate Rupert Brooke, the British poet who died on the island.

There is also the Church of Agios Athanasios built in the 17th century in the vicinity of the main

Square. A further 10 minutes walk from the city center takes you to the Church of Agios Konstantinos and you can also climb up to the peak of hillock to enthrall yourself with the bewitching panoramic delights of the Mediterranean coastline.

Apart from the beautiful lush green scenery, the village is also famous for its traditional taverns, local ouzeries that allow tourists to quench their thirst any time they want to.

The End

Made in United States
Cleveland, OH
12 May 2025